ESSAYS

ON

SOCIAL SUBJECTS

ESSAYS

ON

SOCIAL SUBJECTS

FROM THE SATURDAY REVIEW

"That man sat down to write a book to tell the world what the world had all his life been telling him."

BOSTON
TICKNOR AND FIELDS
1865

University Press:
Welch, Bigelow, and Company,
Cambridge.

ADVERTISEMENT.

THE following Essays by a Contributor to the "Saturday Review" are reprinted without alteration. Though not inserted in the order of their first appearance, no system of arrangement has been attempted; nor is system practicable, where the only connection between different subjects is to be found in all being treated from the point of view of a single writer's personal experience.

CONTENTS.

Busy People.

IT is fortunate for the mass of mankind that their time is pretty well laid out for them. They are spared the problem which must constantly vex the souls of men, — busy men, not impelled by sheer necessity, — what is to come of their work, and why they do it. The man who ploughs or carpenters sees a satisfactory fruit of his labors. He knows that the world could not get on without him, that he, as one of a class, is perfectly indispensable to the well-being, the existence even, of mankind. That we must work, and that, because we must, something useful will be provided for us to do, every believer in a Providence cannot but assume. But people who idolize work of their own devising, — a common form of worship in our time, — are inevitably subject to self-delusions. Very few men who work with their brains, who invent work of any kind for themselves, can, in fact, be as sure that they are benefiting their species as the man who weaves or digs. Many authors unquestionably are serving their generation, many philanthropists, many preachers, many philosophers, many — let us say — essayists and critics; but the mere dignity of the sphere and the conviction of utility, though self-sustaining, do not of themselves prove it. In fact, the higher the aim, the less confident should men be of the result. We are commanded to work, work is an instinct, and head-work in a certain sense is a higher form of work than hand-work; and the individual plods on, trusting to these general truths. But except where there is an abiding afflatus, — an outpouring which a man must utter or die, — except a man is habitually "overflowing as the moon at the full," it may almost be doubted whether literary work could be carried on by modest men without the common tie which makes all laborers one brotherhood, — that they earn money by it. Money is something positive, a reason for exertion apart from the sense of the value of your work. Your work may not be good, even in your own eyes; it may not teach or prove, or edify or amuse; but the idea of wages reduces the pen to the instrument of an honest trade, and the wielder of it to the condition of an honest laborer. He is not oppressed by the humbling sense of shame or failure, by the sore misgiving that he is spinning worthless cobwebs out of his own vitals, only for the remorseless housewife Oblivion to sweep away; for if he does not serve society, it serves him. Something comes of the transaction; which cannot always be said of the mere fancy work done for honor and glory, or even for the gratuitous benefit of the human species. We believe the world of writers, on whom men rely for their daily supply of teaching and amusement, would be "utterly consumed by sharp distress" at the emptiness and vanity of their work, but for the sedative and consoling reflection that they are day-laborers, and write for their hire, and therefore may flatter themselves, by analogy with their brethren of the plough and loom, that what is fairly paid for is worth having, and that what is worth paying for must have some intrinsic worth. If there is a fallacy, it is decently hid. Under it the husbandry of the brain is still carried on, and a precarious crop harvested.

We doubt whether work should be so very delightful to the worker as it seems to be to some people. A little enthusiasm now and then carries him pleasantly forward, and habit makes it bearable and comparatively easy. But for the brow to sweat is not in the nature of things agreeable, though we feel the better for it, perhaps, when it is cool again. Whenever the mere process of work becomes a man's highest pleasure we suspect something wrong, some deficiency. He ought to be glad when it is over. He ought not to undertake it but with some feeling of necessity, — something impelling him slightly against the grain. Liberty ought to seem greater and better than compulsion, even deliberate self-compulsion. Whenever people set their heads to constant work we may be perfectly certain that they are losing more than they gain, that they are sinking in the scale at once of meditative and social beings, and that the world profits not at all by the overplus of activity.

Perhaps excessive activity and laboriousness is not a very common form of self-mismanagement, but still the work of the world is not done with a wise economy. Some do not work at all, — are utterly lazy. Some do their share grudgingly and unwillingly without giving it their energies; and some are always grinding. They are possessed with the idea that work is virtue and achievement, and renovation and life, that every time they sit still and fold their hands, the wheels of the universe drag heavily, that there is a stop, that mischief and decay are intervening somewhere, and that, till they move again, all nature is out of joint. It is a cheerful notion, no doubt, that we are necessary to the well-being and harmony of things, if this conviction goes along with the persuasion that the sort of work we turn out is commensurate with the mighty need: and work has, no doubt — a man's own work, if he keeps his mind pretty exclusively upon it — the power of magnifying itself. Very few people, indeed, can embrace the idea that they are of no use; even their existence implies to most people the necessity for their existence; but the busy man, mixed up in all sorts of affairs, with a finger in every pie, and always comparing his brisk indefatigableness with the indolence of colleagues, or the sloth which does not even undertake labor, comes inevitably to put a high value on what he does, and to think it essential and necessary.

Yet, really, an immense proportion of labor of this sort must be superfluous. Only a percentage, to speak in mercantile phrase, can reach the case. There is boundless waste in mere unassisted intellectual industry. We must work trusting that some one of the thousand seeds we sow will take root; and often good comes where we least rely on it. But we suspect human nature is not strong enough to bear the sense of failure which would be felt if the actual fruit of our exertions, the miserable gleanings of so much promise, were revealed to us; if all that came, for instance, of one busy day's speeches, meetings, lectures, books, articles, hurryings to and fro, runnings hither and thither, all that makes such mighty stir in the doing, were set before us. We admit that ignorance is probably bliss in this case, and we will not pursue the subject; for after all, if the busy workers do comparatively little good, the lazy do none, and ruin themselves into the bargain. But such considerations, while they ought not to interfere with work as a duty, may check it as a monomania. The man who has no time for his friends, who has to apportion his day into fragments which fit into one another like a Chinese puzzle, whose whole scheme is disturbed by a moment's interruption, who suffers under every accidental hinderance, who hurries from one engagement to another, who at every compulsory check or failure feels himself wasting and looks out for something to fill the gap, will perhaps do well now and then to ask what is the good of it all? and who would be the loser if he condescended to a little relaxation? If, in the unwilling holiday, he discovers that he has lost the power of enjoyment, that his social instincts have failed him, that free thought has dwindled, that a thousand interests are lost to him because he can only care where self is bustling and moiling and feeling itself important, then the check will have taught him a useful lesson. No man can be always busy without being slavishly busy. "The most active or busy man," Bacon tells us, "that hath been or can be, hath no question many vacant times of leisure, while he expecteth the tides and returns of business, except he be either tedious and of no despatch, or lightly and unworthily ambitious to meddle with things that might be better done by others." But if, indeed, he is so involved that relaxation is unattainable, then he may rely on it that society is treating him shabbily, employing him as its dependent on routine work, trusting to fresher minds, to men capable of leisure, its more responsible errands, and reserving for them its real gratitude and rewards. While he thinks himself a martyr to its service, it considers the favors really on its own side. It is humoring a propensity and furnishing employment for a blind instinct, and when he looks for any return he will find disappointment, and hear himself put off with the old retort, — "No thanks to him; if he had no business he would have nothing to do."

Our remarks of course do not apply to men of business as such. Few men who apply themselves strictly to their own calling are overworked in the way we mean. There is always a propensity to take things easily where the idea of supererogation is wanting; and the man who prides himself on never passing westward of Temple Bar, and who is set up as a model tradesman, a pattern of clockwork punctuality and concentrated energies, will be found to spend a good many hours of every day in mere gossip and newspaper reading. For, in fact, men's capacity for labor is limited, if by labor we mean an intelligent application of the powers to any work in hand. It is an exercise of patience on this account to watch the progress of skilled labor of any sort. The bricklayer, the gardener, the mechanic are so deliberate in every movement, — each act is so surrounded and saturated, as it were, in waiting and leisure, — that the observer longs to snatch the tool out of their hands and do the job for them; and very likely he could do it in half the time; but after the exertion he would rest on his laurels. The day-laborer, who has ten or twelve hours of it, only takes his repose in minute, inglorious instalments. People who contend too resolutely against this natural drag on progress, who will work faster than the speed to which their capabilities limit them, defeat their own ends. They are borne along by mere senseless impetus, and their work either remains a defect and a hinderance, or has to be undone and retraced.

We suspect that our age is particularly prolific of this sort of busy men, as supplying a wide field for them from the great increase of public business and joint exertion. Where men once worked solitarily in their closets in personal effort, they now work in committees, boards, and other associations, thus reversing the old arrangement, which was to labor alone, and to enjoy leisure in company. It must be owned people had then but a narrow acceptation of the word "neighbor," it was every man for himself and his friend, not for himself and the wide world. But the effect of this limitation rendered it impossible for any given man to have so many irons in the fire as the active temperament finds room for now; and so the workers, as well as the wits, had a jolly time of it. They were idle men after two or three o'clock of the day, — the previous hours, well applied, serving for most men's private affairs, — and they supped nightly in company. If people were to return to this sort of life now, we should expect a universal collapse. That things went on at all, nay, that there was actual progress all the while, is a proof that the seething excitement of apparent work in our own day is not all productive, that a great deal of it simply supplies employment; in fact, is working in a circle. And this brings us to our real ground of quarrel with the over-busy habit of mind, which is, that it not only spoils a man for society, but stops all real progress and cultivation of his own mind. It imprisons him in himself, and shuts him out from a whole range of good and happy influences; and this not because he works, but because exclusive devotion to his own efforts makes him set an undue value upon them and upon himself. The position is a false and mistaken one.

> "The man whose eye
> Is ever on himself, doth look on one
> The least of nature's works";

and yet this is inevitably the attitude of one who prefers his own work to intercourse with others, and who thinks he must impart all and can receive nothing. His whole demeanor shows it. His bustle is a constant reproof, his uniform plea of want of time a standing insult.

We pity men who, while esteeming themselves the benefactors and regenerators of their species, awake a certain resentment above and beyond that inevitable consequence of self-estimation, being thought bores. And this feeling of society will seem to them all the harder and more unthankful, in that it certainly likes busy women. A certain fuss of occupation fits in with their place and nature. Their work looks natural, and has never a touch of reproof in it, which man's fussiness always has. A man cannot be busy without a certain ostentation; but a woman may be in a little commotion from morning till night, occupied with her needle, with her household, her studies, her accomplishments, even with her schools and amongst her poor; and instead of exciting our spleen, if she manage well, we feel, as it were, sleeping partners in her labors, and by some mysterious soothing process to have a share in the merit of them. But a busy woman who is always otherwise engaged when she is wanted, — who keeps her husband waiting for dinner, — who talks with solemn prolixity of her schemes and doings, how she labors, how much depends upon her, — who delights in being overdriven, — who describes herself as in a turmoil of business, and is forever parading her own hobbies, — is perhaps the greater bore of the two, for she is the greater contradiction to the ideal woman, as being uncomfortable and irritating. She is worrying where worry is least looked for, and is therefore the greater hardship. But there are not many such women. They figure in books rather than in actual life; and so much is occupation congenial to women, that even this is better than doing nothing. Society does not assume for them that background of hard work which gives to men's social idleness the pretence of relaxation; and thus listlessness, inactivity, and folding of the hands in women is a painful anomaly to their idlest male friends, and acts upon them like a cold hearth or lukewarm coffee. In fact, it is unpretending or trifling employments that should be made prominent. We should not have quarrelled with Will Whimble for parading his tobacco-stoppers, dog-whips, or fishing-tackle, in all companies, any more than we do now with the ladies for putting forward their netting and embroidery; but men should be diffident, modest, reserved, retiring about their real work, the labor of hand and brain, of soul and spirit, because it is a venture, because they should know something of their own weaknesses, and because far-off results alone can show the value of their work, or whether it has a value beyond the occupation, stimulus, and interest it has furnished to their own minds.

SNUBBING.

WHAT is that thing which everybody remembers, which in the most grateful of us outlives all benefits and overtops all services? How may a man construct himself a niche in every mind, connect undying associations with his name, haunt innumerable memories, make himself a household word, point a moral, and become a standing illustration? How may he get himself thought of and talked of most lastingly and surely? The answer is really too obvious. Simply by cultivating the art of snubbing, or, in favored instances, by merely withdrawing all checks on a natural bias and yielding to the dictates of an inborn acidity. It is an old word, and was very appropriately used in other days to express the withering action of the east wind; but we make no apology for using it in its modern and more familiar sense, as a social blight, as nipping our budding joys, and breathing its cold blast on human jollity. And yet what is a snub, after all, that it should brand itself so indelibly? Why should we be more vulnerable to its attacks than to more formidable thrusts? If it were anything very seriously touching character or credit, it would not go by that name. The word affects to be humorous, and the wound is assumed to be slight, and men are not unused to plain speaking: they acquiesce in the rights of authority in others; and youth, which is especially sensitive to snubs — which experiences all the fever fit of shame at being merely told to mind its own business — makes comparatively small account of more serious censure, and indulges in a playful nomenclature for the graver forms of reproof. How does it give more pain than many a heavy rebuke from quarters whose displeasure is serious, considering that the man who snubs does not primarily mean to give pain at all?

There are people who are conscious and proud of the faculty of giving pain, who have a morbid appetite for making people uneasy about them, to whom a comfortable person is an eyesore. They feel the promptings of an impulse akin to that which made the Roman Emperor, seeing a fat and jovial senator enjoying himself in the amphitheatre, bid his attendants put a sword in that man's hand and make him fight a lion; and which stirs in the domestic tyrant —

> "Pluto they called him, and they called him well,
> For 't was no heaven where he was pleased to dwell" —

but there need be nothing cruel in the man who snubs. It is good sort of people who are tempted to it, honest, sincere men, who have a notion of doing their friends good, of disabusing them summarily of their faults, and shaking them out of follies and mistakes; as when Dr. Johnson, the great master of the art, turned upon one of his flatterers: "Sir, you have but two topics, — yourself and me. I am sick of both." They go right at the offence against taste, sense, or propriety, as it may be, and have a confidence in their way of putting things so as to confound and convince the sinner at a stroke. They are alive to two things, — the matter to be exposed and put down, and their aptitude for the work. The feelings of their friend are the only part of the question not taken into account, which, however, happen to be dearer to the patient than either his friend's perspicacity or abstract truth, even though there existed no difference of opinion on this latter point.

When we endeavor to analyze it, the immediate effect of a snub is to induce a feeling of deprivation and exposure. Its physical sensation is like the sudden loss of a garment, and the consequent rush of cold; and we do in fact lose, in the surprise, the snug covering of our usual self-respect. We are dependent creatures. We are apt, on the instant of others not respecting us, to feel ourselves not respectable, small, inferior, incompetent, unable to hold our own; and hence the main annoyance. That which predominates in a snub is the pressing difficulty of how to take it. We are caught at unawares without our weapons. There are assaults and aggressions of a nature to rouse our courage and to quicken our powers, which call for and suggest an answer, which may be resented on the spot without injury to our dignity; but this is not one of them. All that can be done generally under a snub — all, at least, that we actually do — is to pull-up suddenly with an inner blank sense of tingling, a doubt as to where we are, a confused feeling of having the worst of it, which our instinct teaches us to keep to ourselves as much as possible. For it must be noted that a snub is of necessity a sudden blow, given when we are at a disadvantage, careless, and at ease in the security of social intercourse. Social intercourse takes sympathy for granted. It assumes one general genial sentiment, a disposition to follow a lead, to pursue subjects in the spirit in which they are started. A snub is a check, a blank, it is a curtain suddenly drawn down, it is pulling-up against a dead-wall, it is cold obstruction and recoil. Either the snubber has authority on his side, and we have laid ourselves open by some inadvertence, by a misplaced trust in his condescension, — and we have seen parents painfully snub their children in this sort, first allowing them liberties, then stopping them with a harsh check in mid-career of spirits, and this in the presence of strangers, — or, perhaps, we have given way to enthusiasm, and are met by ridicule; or we have made a confidence which we think tender, and it is received with indifference; or we tell a story, and are asked for the point of it; or we are given to understand that we are mistaken where we have assumed ourselves well informed; or our taste is coolly set at naught; or we talk, and are reminded we are prosy; or we are brought face-to-face with our ignorance in a way to make us feel it most keenly. The strength of a snub lies in the sudden apprehension that we have committed ourselves, and a consequent painful sense of insignificance, — that there is somebody quite close to us, regardless of our feelings, looking down on us, and ostentatiously unsympathizing. This is an elaborate description of perhaps a momentary sensation following on an encounter probably as short, after which each party may seem to pursue his way unconscious; but in human affairs time is not the measure of importance, and one of the two at least treasures a memory of it in his heart bearing no proportion whatever to the time it took in acting.

Perfectly collected and self-satisfied persons are impervious to snubs. Sam Weller is represented as receiving one from his master (we need not say well merited) with perfect smiling serenity. So are the happy few gifted with the power of repartee and rejoinder, who may be called social debaters, whose glory is an emergency, who can collect their powers on the instant, and "give the check they take" with usury. When M. Scribe, according to the newspaper story, answered the millionnaire who wanted him to lend him the use of his genius for a consideration, that it was contrary to Scripture for a horse (so he wrote it) and an ass to plough together, it was a perfectly fair snub. The man deserved anything he got, but he must have felt triumph rather than mortification when, on the spur of the moment, he could demand what right had M. Scribe to call him a horse. But these cases are too few to be taken into account, and the practised snubber has generally the game in his own hand, and secures a victory. If morals are his forte, he will have demonstrated how much more prompt are his moral instincts than our own, how quick he is to discover the right which our dulled perceptions or stolid selfishness had missed. If his line is intellectual, he will have reminded us of our illogical habits of thought and our bounded views compared with his keen intelligence and clear judgment. If life and manners are his care, he will have convicted us of mistakes, awkwardnesses, solecisms; if information and general knowledge, he will have succeeded in impressing us with a sense of our deficiencies; if taste, he will take care to show us that there is nothing he values so slightly as our opinion.

That natural human sensitiveness is constantly lost sight of by quick and clever people, is clear even from fiction. In the dialogue of most novels, we find snubs which could not be inflicted in real intercourse without bringing all intercourse to an end. All historical conversations professing to have actually taken place—from Canute's reproof to his courtiers to the "Sir, you don't know the poor figure you make," quoted by Macaulay—foster the delusion that mankind will stand wounds to their self-love which they will not stand; and the snubbers may thus be tempted to try experiments which, in spite of momentary triumphs, end in their own real defeat. There are men exemplary in all the duties of life who never pass a day without snubbing somebody,—their wives, of course (natural victims, used to be told that they say nothing and do nothing right), their children, their servants, their underlings, their acquaintances, their associates. Every day something has passed their lips which has acted like a blow at the time, and worked on the recollection like a blister, which has been repeated with querulous soreness and been passed on to the world as a fresh trait of character, which has added to the growing barrier which daily rises between the man and his species. Not that we can cut him,—we do not even wish to do so. All the ceremonies of friendly intercourse continue to pass between us; there is no reason they should ever be left off. But at every encounter he gets shoved farther and farther away from our secrets. One by one he loses the key to the hearts of his friends, who stand on the defensive, keep watch, shut themselves up in his presence with instinctive caution, till we doubt not he often in his inner heart wonders at his own isolation. For our part we are sincerely sorry for him; and we are so conscious besides that men may have the habit without knowing it, that we would offer one general counsel,—never under any temptation to practise a talent for setting down on people worth caring for. Risk a good deal, take a circuitous route, leave good advice unsaid, or said in less trenchant telling fashion, bear irritations, nuisances, what not, rather than inflict any sudden wound on your friend's self-love. Do not put him, on your behalf, on the duty of Christian forgiveness. Allow him to rest in some ignorance of your opinion, even though he may believe it more to his advantage than it happens to be. Submit to be incomplete; sacrifice the pleasure of being sharp and acute at his expense; for it is very certain that he will not like you the better, and very unlikely also that he should himself *be* the better, for your having made him feel like, and perhaps look like, a fool. If he is often put under the apprehension of it, the least that can be expected of him is, that he will eschew your confidence, and carefully keep on the windy side of intimacy.

Here lies the secret of so many charges of ingratitude, and benefits forgotten, of unrequited, unvalued sacrifices. Not that a few, or even a series, of ill-considered, unpalatable words ought to counterbalance real services, but that they put human nature to a strain which too severely tests its weak points. And there is this to be said,—that contempt, of all things the hardest to bear, is, if we go to the bottom of it, the motive force of most snubs. The practice is certainly incompatible with a respectful habit of mind. Our friend is in a hurry to tell us that our judgment is worth nothing, that our expression of it must be stopped, that we, or something about us, must be put down. As we think over the matter, the examples that first occur come from contemptuous minds, — men without deference, who are accustomed to lean upon themselves, who do not expect to find much in other people. We do not find them appealing to others, or wishing to know their thoughts, or willing to follow out their speculations, or listening to their suggestions. They live and think alone, impatient of interference and interruption, and nourish some notion of themselves which practically, though it may not take the form of vulgar arrogance and vanity, sets them above the possibility of benefit from the crude, unformed, untaught intelligences around them. Indeed, it is their impatience of other men's ideas and conclusions which leads them to commit themselves.

And it is to be observed that such men never do see others at their best. A person of ordinary modesty, not gifted with self-reliance, not confident of his position, cannot show himself to advantage under such circumstances; and thus men are encouraged in their self-esteem by the consequences of their own ungraciousness. Nobody is quite himself before them, unless he is also past the possibility of an open show of contempt, though even this immunity depends on the rank of the snubber. The Duke of Wellington could tell an earl, his colleague, "You are over-educated for your intellect"; and when wit and learning were rank, Warburton and Swift could and did snub all the world. If our remarks lack the pungency of appropriate illustration, it is not because apt examples do not crowd upon us. We could fill columns with them, — the collegiate, the social, the domestic, — all of them very much to the purpose, and some very amusing; but, as we have said, these are just the things people never forget. Disguise them as we would, they would be traced to their right source, and the sanctities of private life must be respected, though our disquisition lose half its value, and all its liveliness, by the sacrifice.

IGNORANCE.

THERE are some sorts of ignorance that are evidently not at all disagreeable to, what we will call, their possessors. Indeed, pride in knowledge might sometimes seem to have given place to pride in ignorance. We are used to hear men boast of knowing nothing on such and such a subject, of being profoundly ignorant on matters which engage the common attention, and of which most people have a smattering; and we have learned to understand, by the obtrusive confession, either that the speaker's time has been better engaged, or that Nature, liberal to him in great things, has inflicted on him some slight defect or incapacity separating him from less gifted men by an idiosyncrasy. Or, it may be, he has such high and superior notions of what constitutes knowledge, that nothing less than entire mastery, amounting to an exclusive possession of a subject, deserves the name, and that everything short of this is ignorance. Again, there is an honest philosophical ignorance which must be rather pleasant, for it comes of clearness of perception. The very ignorance of certain profound thinkers is impressive, and strikes awe. In fact, there is a form of it that only one of this sort can feel. Owing to the lucidity of his thoughts, the keenness of his apprehension in things which he does understand, he is alive to a strange and startling contrast when by chance he falls on anything that puzzles him. He finds himself pulled up; he is sensible of having arrived at the traditional millstone; his reason is consciously at fault, and straightway he lays his finger on the dark spot, and says, "This is ignorance!" In such a confession there can be no shame, in fact, it is not so much he that is ignorant as the human race of which he feels himself the representative. He knows that what man sees he sees, but it is given to him to distinguish with exactness between the light and the obscure; he is agreeably conscious of being, in his own person, a test and gauge of mortal powers, a discoverer of the limits of human thought. And if there is satisfaction in these voyages into unfathomable seas, there is another form of ignorance which surely supplies heartier pleasures still. We do not speak of that "Ignorance which is bliss," for this the child is restlessly bent on exchanging for a painful knowledge, but of that form of ignorance which, never being recognized as such, remains a comfortable life-long companion; the ignorance, emphatically, of the vulgar, that "blind and naked ignorance" which

> "Delivers brawling judgments unashamed
> On all things all day long,"

because, not knowing one thing more or better than another, and being sustained by indomitable self-reliance, it sincerely mistakes its uniformity of defect for general enlightenment, and trusts its intuitions. Again, there is feminine ignorance, recognized on all hands for what it really is, yet held in high esteem as an engine of coquetry and as a conscious fascination. A pretty or a charming woman feels herself more pretty and more charming for not knowing anything hard, deep, or recondite. It costs her nothing to disown the slightest acquaintance with the dead languages, or science, or anything that calls for abstract thought. In the opinion of those whose approval she most cares for, she might as well assume Miss Blimber's spectacles as shine in any one of them.

These forms of ignorance are, however, one and all, remote from our present theme, which is that ignorance of which some of us — how many of us! — are conscious, and which is anything but pleasant. We speak of the ignorance of which we make no parade, which is dragged from us against our will, or unwittingly revealed while our good genius is sleeping, which has been with some of us (till time and experience did their work of reassurance) our skeleton in the closet, which any day might bring to light. For, though never wholly got rid of, it is on the hope and sensitiveness of youth that this pain presses most sorely. In those ingenuous days when the memory still tingles with examinations, when we have not ceased to believe in the knowledge of everybody else, when the phrases, "What every school-boy knows," or "What every school-boy would be birched for not knowing," seem to mean what they say, then it is that we recognize what a shameful thing it is not to know more. Then to stand convicted before our fellow-men of not knowing certain facts, of having perpetrated some gross blunder in what is assumed to be a common heritage of knowledge, is a blot and a slur, and brings with it a sense of disgrace amounting to dishonor. He has missed a very poignant and memorable sensation who has never blushed in secret at some hideous lapse, nor for its sake desired to hide his head from the accusing light of day, realizing in fancy what the Finger of Scorn must mean. In truth, many a young man, not naturally cruel, has heard with a sense of relief of the expatriation or even death of some witness of his shame, — some one before whom, for instance, he has committed himself to an error of some hundred years in a date, or has betrayed confusion about kings and sides in the Wars of the Roses, or confounded the Vedas with the Sagas, or not known the identity of St. Austin with St. Augustine, or has supposed "It must be so," and the rest of it, to come in somewhere in Hamlet's soliloquy, or that Haydn composed the "Messiah," or that Tycho Brahe lived before Sanchoniathon, or has laid bare some extraordinary confusion of his mind about eclipses of the moon. Not that he cares about the Vedas or Sanchoniathon, but it is horrible to be thought ignorant of the things that other people know, or are supposed to know, or that he thinks he once did know, only memory let them slip before it had fairly got hold of them. For the poor memory gets all the blame, as if memory were responsible for what the attention never gave it in charge. Treacherous memory, which with so many of us is responsible for our ignorance! — "with creeping crooked pace," grudging, vacillating, uncertain, playing the part of that Ignaro, "foster-father of the giant dead," —

"That on his staffe his feeble steps did frame,
And guide his weary steps both to and fro,
For his eyesight him failed long ago.
And on his arme a bunch of keys he bore,

> The which, unused, rust did over growe ;
> Those were the keys of every inward dore ;
> But he could not them use, but kept them still in store."

It is certain that in most of us, without any sense of amendment in ourselves, this strong, deep disgust at our ignorance passes with youth. We begin to suspect great barren tracts in everybody's range of information. There are not many people who do not betray a blank in some point where we had assumed them to be well informed. Everybody commits himself in turn, not, perhaps, in the way of conventional ignorance, but in ignorance of matters which it is equally a disgrace not to know. For why should what men learn from books and polished society be the only test? Why is it not as dishonorable to have neglected the use of our eyes? A little experience convinces us that culpable ignorance is not confined to the form of it which most vexes the detected soul. The subject takes a more general form, apart from our consciousness, and one which we can contemplate very much at our ease.

It is indeed wonderful how little some people contrive to learn of things that it does not seem easy to help knowing, and it makes general progress the more surprising when we consider how little it has been helped on by the mass of mankind. The great proportion of those that live in towns, and have before them all their lives the processes of building, the distinctions of architecture, the suggestive hum of machinery, the varieties of merchandise, the profusion of markets, are dead and blind not only to all that these things teach, but to what is obtruded on their eyes if it does not immediately concern their own wants and vanities. Nor does the country tell them more. They will not know from what hills the stream that waters their fields has its source, or towards what river it flows, or what counties and villages it passes by. They cannot distinguish the note of the birds that have sung to them since they were born. They have discovered nothing for themselves of the habits of beasts or insects that have haunted their path or forced themselves on their regard from childhood. They do not know the flowers at their feet, nor the outline of the horizon their eye ever rests on. We verily believe that there are a good many highly educated people who could not for the life of them recall the outline of a cow or a sheep without ludicrous blunders. Why is not all this universal knowledge? Why are the people who notice what comes before them to be marked by a separating name and called naturalists? Why are we ashamed of a failure in what comes to us through books and the costly instrumentality of masters and teachers, — why do we blush at any flagrant slip in history, or science, or language, —

and keep cool and easy under any extravagance of error in what nature, through our own observation, might teach us? There are, no doubt, plenty of answers, still it is a question.

In contemplating the general ignorance, and the popular injustice as to what constitutes reprehensible ignorance, we thus grow less sensitive towards our own. Also, be it added, there are forms of it which inevitably grow upon us. There are a vast number of things which we knew as boys, and have forgotten now, and we perceive that the knowledge and the ignorance are much on a par. It was a knowledge of mere words, an imposture, fertilizing neither heart nor brain; we feel that, if it had entered into either, it would have remained with us; or, being genuine knowledge, though no longer at our fingers' ends, it may yet have done its work, and contributed something to what there is good in us. Unquestionably, the mind that has learnt things and forgotten them is on a wholly different and superior footing from that which has never received the teaching. Thus most things learnt may be intended to be partially forgotten in everything but the training they have given. Cultivation is certainly consistent with a great deal of ignorance, if the constant confession, "I do not know," is to be the criterion.

In another respect, too, we learn to take our individual ignorance coolly. We find we can fairly keep it out of sight by a constant exercise of caution, and a sort of involuntary finesse which is itself an education. Society generally is up to the fact that the polite assumption of universal knowledge in all its members *is* an assumption. No well-bred person will put it to the test. We do now and then come upon a questioner, a self-elected social inspector, who does by society what a malignant school inspector does by a class, — lay himself out to find, not what they *do* know, but what they do *not.* But society is up in arms, and makes common cause against such disturbers of its smooth equanimity. How differently does the polite example of that *lusus naturæ*, the thoroughly well-informed man, show himself! He takes for granted, not in hypocrisy, but through mere genial good-nature and desire for sympathy, some share of his own gifts in every one he meets. "Everybody knows a little Arabic," we once heard a pleasant man of this sort say in a mixed company, to account for his being able to converse in that language. It was a *bonâ fide,* though, as it proved, ill-founded assumption, which he would have been very far from putting to the proof, but which gave every one a little flavor of Arabic while the conceit lasted. In the next place, we find that the ignorance of which youth is so sensitive is not the barrier it was supposed to be. The world is not governed by those who know the most, nor is it what men know, but what they do, that determines their place in the world. How much ignorance, for example, is daily displayed by our leading journalists? If, by chance, we happen to have real information on some subject on which their graceful sentences flow so easily, we shall certainly detect error or misstatement, — not intentional, but the result of ignorance. The writer is out in some important particulars. There is a general air of familiarity with the subject, of knowing what he is about; but we see that he goes on assumptions for want of knowing the facts. And yet the world would much rather receive its impressions from a man who writes well than from an expert dryly up in his one theme; and perhaps wisely, for the ignorance of the practised writer is tempered by large general experience, which preserves him from flagrant blunders, and may, likely enough, assist him to an approach to the truth sufficient for general purposes. We are sure that, with some skilled confident writers of this class, an ignorance which throws them upon their own resources is better for their purpose than half-knowledge, — always an uncertain, halting, hesitating guide, which simply puts them off the scent of instinct.

Intense as is the shame of convicted ignorance

under certain conditions, there is still a delightful source of relief to the ingenious mind in a frank confession, in making a clean breast of it, in revealing blanks, smirches, confusions of memory, and even startling deficiencies in the matter of "what everybody knows," in showing ourselves to some sympathizing hearer (he must be sympathizing) just as we are. But if this self-portraiture is not to our mind, and our ignorance in certain fashionable points of knowledge presses on us, the thing to do is to get up some subject of which we stand a chance of being sole student in our own circle. It matters not how trifling the specialty, if a man only knows something that nobody else knows, the world will respect him. Only be an authority upon beetles, or even sea-weeds, and you may have small Latin and less Greek, you may know nothing of literature, and be grossly in the dark on politics, and it may all tend to your honor. If you know absolutely nothing else, how much you must know about beetles! It is a case of concentration of the powers, of force of will, of single aim, of that ardent, indomitable pursuit of knowledge which is passion. And this is, perhaps, only a caricature of the truth, — a truth of which, in an age of new sciences and perpetual discoveries, it is a comfort to be reminded, — that a wise man must, after all, be content to be ignorant of many things.

FOOLISH THINGS.

THE subject of folly is a wide one. Mr. Buckle's sixteen volumes would hardly exhaust its various manifestations; what, then, can be expected in a single page? But it is also attractive. Nobody is disinclined to have his belief in the universality of folly confirmed by a new instance, every one is ready to speculate on the motive or want of motive of ridiculous human action. But the foolish things we have here set ourselves to speak of are not attractive. They furnish food for anything rather than amused supercilious analysis. Are there any of our readers who never in their own persons say or do foolish things, — who are never conscious of having been deserted by their good genius? If there are, we do not write for them. It is one's own foolish things which at present engage our attention, for which we assume the sympathy of fellow-feeling, and reckon on touching an answering chord in other breasts not a few. We are not speaking now of grave errors and mistakes, but of the inadvertencies, weaknesses, and follies which haunt our subordinate, social, man-fearing conscience; which we may not know to have been perceived by any but ourselves, but which nevertheless affect us, not because they are wrong, but silly, and because they may be thought more silly by others even than by ourselves, which leave a sense of self-betrayal, making us ask in bitterness, —

> "Who shall be true to us
> When we are so unsecret to ourselves?"

They are the things which allow us to go to sleep at night with an undisturbed conscience, but wake us with a start hours before the dawn, and set us wondering, — How could I make such a fool of myself? Where was the impulse to that vain show-off? What could have induced me to talk of such a one, — to confide my private concerns to So-and-so? For it may be noted that sins of omission play but a small part in this periodical tragedy. It is not lost opportunities, but heedless, ill-considered speech and action, that fret us at unseasonable hours, — some thoughtless license of the tongue, perhaps, or some passing vanity leading to misplaced confidence and weak reliance on sympathy. In the young, the fear of presumption is a fruitful yet innocent source of these stings of memory. Young people are sometimes made uneasy for days from the notion of having committed some unwarrantable familiarity, which under excitement seemed, and very likely was, perfectly natural.

We are advised to sleep upon certain designs, but it means really to wake upon them. Nothing is more curious than the revulsion a short interval makes in our whole view of things, — no magic more bewildering than the transmutations which a few hours of insensibility produce, — a few hours of being thrown absolutely upon ourselves. What an idea it gives us of the effect of association, of the action of man upon man! Nobody can allow himself to be real and natural in his intercourse with others, and at the same time act as he laid himself out beforehand to act, or as he wishes (we may too often say), on looking back, that he had acted. If this is true in the solemn and weighty affairs of life, it must of necessity be true in the light or less responsible contact of society, where the little turns and accidents of the hour are constantly throwing us off our rules, and tempting us to ventures and experiments. All wit, all repartee, all spontaneous effervescence of thought and fancy, are of the nature of experiment. All new unplanned revelations of self, — all the impulses, in fact, which come of collision with other minds in moments of social excitement, whether pleasurable or irritating, — are apt to leave qualms and misgivings on the sensitive and reflective temperament. Thus, especially, sins against taste fret us in the heavy yet busy, excitable hour which we have fixed on for the levee of these spectres, when our thoughts, like hounds, scent out disagreeable things with a miraculous instinct, drag them to light, fly from subject to subject, however remote and disconnected, and hem us round with our own peccadilloes. Society in the cold dawn looks on us as a hard taskmaster, exacting, unrelenting, seeing everything, taking account of everything, forgetting nothing, judging by externals, and holding its judgments irreversible. For, after all, it is a cowardly time. We are not concerning ourselves now with *bonâ fide* penitence, but only with its shadow and imitation, — a fear of what people will think, a dread of having committed ourselves, whose best alleviation lies in empty resolutions of dedicating the coming day to a general reversal or reparation of yesterday, to a laborious mending and patching, which is to leave us sadder and wiser men; along with a certain self-confidence (also the offspring of the hour), that if we can only set the past to rights, rectify, explain, recant effectually, our present experience will preserve us from all future recurrence of even the tendency and temptation to do foolish things. We own this to be cowardly. It is fortunate that we cannot mould ourselves on the model of these morbid regrets; for the influences which make us seem to ourselves so different in the rubs of domestic and social life from our solitary selves — so that we are constantly taking ourselves by surprise — are not all bad ones. They may be more unselfish than those which impel to remorse, and make us feel so sore against ourselves. There is a certain generous throwing of one's self into the breach in some crisis, whether grave or gay, which often brings us to grief. There is a certain determined devotion to the matter in hand, — a resolution, come what may, to carry a thing through, — which is better than caution, though by no means a subject for self-congratulation at five o'clock in the morning; or, indeed, so long as it lives in the memory at all. On the whole, it is better as it is. We are gainers in freedom by living in a world where it is possible to commit ourself, — to go beyond intentions, — to be impulsive, incautious. If everybody were as self-possessed, as much on his guard as we wish we had been in these periods of harassed meditation, society would not be a very refreshing or invigorating sphere.

This is a surer source of consolation, as far as our observation goes, than any argument from analogy that our fears delude us. If we look round on those of our friends whose prudence we can scarcely hope to equal, far less to surpass, — whom we trust for manner, discretion, and judgment, — there is scarcely one who does not now and then disappoint or surprise us by some departure from his usual right way of thinking and acting, by committing some moral or social solecism, just one of the things to haunt the first waking hour. We are not meaning merely *clever* people, for cleverness has a prescriptive right to do foolish things, but wise and sensible people who have a rule of action, and habitually go by it, — habitually, but not always; — and a foolish thing done or said by a wise man certainly stands out with a startling prominence and distinctness, pointing out the weak place there is in the best of us. When our wise friend, under some malignant influence, says or does something exceptionally silly, the thing assumes a sort of life from contrast. It is quoted against him, and, perhaps, in some quarters a permanently lower estimate of mind and character is the consequence. Do the same things that in this case strike us strike the perpetrator? Can a wise man say a foolish thing and remain forever unconscious of it? One thing we must believe, — it cannot be only a latent self-conceit in the midst of our humiliations and self-reproaches that leads us to assume them not universal. There are people so uniformly foolish, so constantly impertinent, rash, talkative, unsecret, or blundering, that, if revisited by their errors, solitude would be one long penance which could not fail to tell upon their outer aspect. The fool *par excellence* is not, we gladly believe, haunted by his folly. It is when we have departed from our real character, when our instincts have failed us, when we have gone against ourselves, that we writhe under these tormenting memories.

The subject is worth dwelling upon for one reason. If, with the exception of conspicuous fools, we could realize that this class of regrets are not due to our particular idiosyncrasy, but are a common scourge of weak, vain, irritable, boasting humanity, it ought to conduce to charity in our judgments. If we could believe that the people we dislike suffer these penances, and could give them credit for waking with a twinge an hour earlier than usual, under the remembrance of impertinence, vanity, unkindness, persuaded that certain definite offences against our taste and feeling would haunt their solitary walk and make the trial of their day, we could not but learn patience and toleration. But we are apt to regard our annoyance as the penalty of an exceptionally sensitive social conscience. We and the people we care for cannot do foolishly without feeling sorry for it, — without going through the expiation of a pang; but the people we dislike are insensible, coarse, obtuse, dull, and brutish. Theirs has not been a mistake, which implies a departure from their nature, but an acting up to it and according to it. They are, therefore, showing themselves as they are when they show themselves most unpleasant and repulsive.

Another mode of reconciling ourselves to this prompt Nemesis of minor follies is that it may possibly preserve us from greater ones. It may both imply caution, and keep our caution in practice and repair. We have already made an exception in favor of fools; but are people subject to rash impulses, — impulses swaying their whole destiny and the fate of others, — who find a pleasure in staking the future on some unconsidered chance, — ever visited by regrets for having merely exposed themselves in no more weighty matter than some foolish breach of confidence or lapse of propriety? Are people habitually unguarded ever visited by lesser remorse? Is not this rather a conflict where habitual caution is every now and then betrayed by counter influences? Does a man who is always boasting ever remember any particular boast with a pang? Does one who is always betraying secrets, and revealing his own and other people's privacy, — always talking of himself, always maudlin, always ill-natured or sarcastic, — ever writhe under the recollection of his follies? It is hard to be lenient towards some people, however much it is our duty to think the best.

But whatever tenderness may be shown towards foolish things, acted or spoken, whatever beneficent purpose may be assigned to them in the social economy, our leniency ends here. Little can be said ethically, and nothing prudentially, for foolish things written, — for outbreaks of our follies and tempers on paper; and yet what a fruitful source of these regrets has the pen been with some of us! And never has the sting been sharper than when we realize that our imprudence is in black and white, beyond our reach, irrevocable. The pen gives us a power of having our say out which speech seldom does. We are free from the unaccountable, almost solemn, control that man in bodily presence has over man. Fresh from some injury, we have the plea, the retort, the reproof, the flippancy, the good things in our hands without danger of interruption. We will write it while the subject is fresh and vivid, and the arguments so clear that our correspondent cannot fail of being struck, persuaded, crushed by them. In the heat of composition we foresee those cooler, cautious hours in the distance, and defy them. We have a dim notion that we are doing a foolish thing, but we will act while conviction is supreme, and we send off our letter — to repent sometimes how bitterly!

It has been cleverly said that the whole folly of this proceeding lies, not in the writing, which is an excellent valve to the feelings, but in the sending; and certainly very few letters, written under immediate provocation, would be sent if the writers slept a night upon them. But the pen can do foolish things — things below the writer's standard of speech and action — without provocation. There are many people whose intellect and judgment would stand much higher in the world's estimation if they had never been taught to write. Men write letters and women write notes in total neglect of the rules which guide their conversation, and which win them sometimes an extraordinary reputation for good sense. A whole swarm of absurd impulses cluster round the pen, which leave them alone at other times. A propensity for interference and giving advice is one of these, a passion for explanations, a memory for old grievances, and a faith in the efficacy of formal, prolix, minute statements of wrong, along with querulous hints, unpalatable suggestions, and insinuations generally; all of which are foolish, because they cannot, in the nature of things, have a good issue, and flow from the ready pen in oblivion of obvious consequences, which elsewhere hold the writer in salutary check. Indeed, the pen often wakes a set of feelings which are not known to exist without it. If we must be foolish sometimes, let us then give our folly as short a term as possible. If it must leave traces behind, our memory is a better and safer archive than our enemy's or even our friend's writing-table. Therefore, if any warning of the fit is granted, if a man have any reason for misgivings, let him, before all things, beware of pen and ink. Things are seldom quite hopeless till they are committed to paper, — a scrape is never at its worst till it has given birth to a correspondence.

False Shame.

MR. DICKENS'S story of "Great Expectations" illustrates a certain temper of mind which is perhaps a characteristic of our age. Pip, from the time of his introduction to Estella, is the victim of false shame. Her contempt for the manners of the common boy forced on her companionship, curdled the milk of human kindness in him. Naturally affectionate, from that moment a shadow comes between him and his friend and protector to whom he owed everything, but who had taught him to call the Knave "Jack." What Estella is likely to think interferes with what he ought to think; and gratitude slowly but inevitably yields before the new influence. The picture is, on the whole, a true one. So far as we can realize Pip's situation at all, we can understand his temptations, and acknowledge that his was the very character, or no-character, to fall under them. But, indeed, false shame has not always so much to say for itself as in this instance. Pip is taken from the forge and made a gentleman, a member of what is technically called society,—so at least Mr. Dickens intends us to understand it. Now, undoubtedly, people do owe something to the class for which they have been trained and to which they belong; and if Pip is a gentleman, the honestest, truest-hearted blacksmith in the world, especially if addicted to Joe Gargery's system of expression, must be an awkward appendage. It is more easy to be shocked at Pip's ingratitude than to know precisely what he ought to have done with his brother-in-law. However, we see he is intended to represent one of the vices of society, and we recognize his fitness for the part in a general want of force and stamina, and a predominance of the imagination over the judgment.

Though we call it hard names, it would still be almost a discourtesy to assume our readers to be ignorant of the sensation of false shame, by which we mean shame the fruit of vanity and imagination; for never to have known it is, in our imperfect state, to be without the kindred quality of which it is the abuse,— sensitiveness, a want which would argue bluntness of feeling and dulness of perception. Occasional fits of false shame—of being unreasonably perturbed at circumstances we cannot alter, that are not of our own making, that have nothing in them of which we ought, in strict reason, to be ashamed—have visited most of us. They belong to civilization as opposed to the more primitive forms of society,—to a state of existence where different interests clash, where social and domestic ties may, and do, interfere with one another. Young people, on their first admission to this outer world, are especially afflicted by false shame; so that it may be regarded as one of the moral diseases of the mind's infancy. It is at the bottom of a great deal of their shyness. They cannot feel at ease, because they mistrust something about themselves or their belongings, and have that feeling of bareness and exposure in the presence of unfamiliar eyes which attaches to sensitiveness under untried circumstances. Everything then assumes a magnified, exaggerated character, the place they occupy on the one hand, and the importance of the occasion on the other. The present company is the world, the universe, a convention of men and gods, all forming a deliberate and irreversible judgment upon them, and deciding to their disadvantage on account of some oddness, or awkwardness, or passing slip in themselves or in the accessories about them. But, in most persons, time and experience bring so much humility as teaches them their insignificance. It is not, we soon learn, very likely that at any given time a mixed assemblage is thinking very much about us; and then the horror of a conspicuous position loses its main sting. This on the one hand; on the other, we are not as dependent on the award of society as we were. Even a roomful comprises, to our enlarged imagination, by no means the whole creation. There is something worth caring for outside those walls. And also we have come to form a sort of estimate of ourselves. There is now a third party in the question, in the shape of self-respect. We realize that we are to ourselves of immeasurably more consequence than any one else can be to us. Thus, either by reason or by the natural hardening and strengthening process of the outer air, most people overcome any conspicuous display of the weakness. By the time youth is over, they have either accepted their position or set about in a business-like way to mend it.

But there are some people who never get over this disorder of the faculties, — who are always its victims, — who live in a habitual state of subservience, — who defer perpetually to some opinion, or supposed opinion, which they respect more than their own, and under which they crouch, whether it be that of an individual, a clique, or the world. The sanction of their own judgment is no guaranty; it is powerless unsupported by society's good word. If a man after twenty, or at latest twenty-five, will harp in all companies on his red hair, or be perpetually reminding people that he is little, or embarrass them by allusions to his plebeian birth, or be making absurd apologies for his relations, or depreciate the dinner he has set before his guests, we have not much hope of him. He fails in the quality which defies and puts to flight false shame. He may be wise, he may be witty, he may have the clearest head, the most fluent tongue, the readiest pen; but he wants manliness. The fears, flusters, and perturbations of false shame are a sign of some inherent discrepancy between his intellect and his moral nature which will always keep him immature. Undue compliance with either the social or domestic instinct produces the same effect. Whether a man sacrifices himself by a superstitious worship of public opinion or of private affection, the result is the same. He may stultify himself as effectually by an excessive devotion to his mother and sisters as by a like devotion to Mrs. Grundy; but our concern is with the latter devotee, who lives in fear of being singular, who suspects all closely allied to him of some misfit or incongruity. He is pretty certain to accomplish his own forebodings; for such men are sure to do odd things, as people must who think constantly whether everything they do is according to rule, not what is convenient to do. All our natural actions are done without thought, and we can make breathing a difficulty by thinking about it.

A person under this thraldom, whatever his disposition, will never be of the use he might be to his friends, while he presents an easy mark to his enemies. No one is safe from being thrown over by a friend who makes the world his bugbear; for, whatever the justice of his own perceptions, the opinion which he dreads, and which influences him, is an inferior one. There is actually no limit to such a dependence; it bows before every standard, irrespective of all capacity or right to judge. Whoever can use the weapon of contempt is formidable. Such a man is a prey to the insolence of footmen; he trembles before the tribunal of the servants' hall, and dreads the criticism of his butler, whose definition of a gentleman — of what is expected of a gentleman, of what a gentleman ought and ought not to do — he practically accepts in preference to his own. All this is essentially demoralizing. In fact, no benefits can secure a man of this sort, no ties can bind him, under a particular form of trial; and this not at all from baseness of nature, but because he wants a man's generous self-reliance, — that quality which the weak and the dependent learn to trust, and which gives to manliness a value for which no intellectual excellence whatever is an equivalent. All people are, of course, in a considerable measure, guided in their ways of thinking by general consent, — as, being members of a community, they must be; but there is, beyond this, a slavery in which its victim stands as it were unrepresented in the world's parliament. Few errors bring less reward with them. Nobody likes a coward; and a careless indifference, or even defiance, of popular usage is often taken for a sign of superiority. Human nature is not so hard and cynical as the theory of false shame assumes it to be; and the world is much more good-natured than men of this temper give it credit for. It can discriminate, and sympathize, and tolerate exceptions from its ordinary standard. As no phantoms are so monstrous as the fears of a mind which abandons itself to the apprehensions of false shame, so no predicament or dilemma of actual existence has the pangs and stings which a busy fancy conjures up in anticipation, — just as most disagreeable things are not, when the time comes, as disagreeable as we expected.

There is a hardened class of self-seekers who override all considerations to attain their end, to gratify a low ambition, and get on in the world, — people whom Mr. Dickens again portrays in his Mr. Bounderby, — with whom the genuine victim of false shame must not be confounded. His conscience does not sleep, but his fancy predominates. He owes his uneasiness to his susceptible nature, to the rapidity of his flights, quick to conjure up scenes, and prolific of imaginary contingencies. We may despise the weakness, but must pity its victim as the main sufferer. Indeed, in some cases it would be easy to trace a whole career changed by it. Advantages of education are lost, friendships checked, opportunities shunned, and habits of moody self-contemplation induced at the age when action, the spirit of adventure, and the excitement of new impressions are at their highest in the more healthy and strong temperament; and this not by any means wholly from the sufferer's own fault, but because adverse circumstances, which vigorous and less contemplative minds shake off or bend to their will, tell with such blighting force on more sensitive characters. Writers of modern fiction often show such suspicious familiarity with the workings of false shame that it is easy to suppose the ranks of authors may receive some valuable additions through its paralyzing influence, unfitting men as it does to take that stand in the world of action which their intellect might claim for them. The fashionable novel, a development of modern society, has heretofore done much to create or to foster the feeling. People no longer young bear witness to the singular impression which those pictures made upon a crude, uninformed fancy, — to the discontent they engendered in the childish mind for the dull or homely circumstances of actual life. Nothing could be more frivolous and merely external than the tests of superiority and refinement set up by those arbiters of manners and social standing; but for these very reasons they were more within the compass of a young raw apprehension. The best corrective (not to speak here of the moralist's grave antidotes) was the romantic class of fiction contemporary with and succeeding to the Almacks school, which took the opposite line altogether. In tales of this order, characters over whom the domestic affections do not tyrannize are represented as mere monsters, and are treated without mercy. Our readers will remember that in "Undine," which so bewitched our youth, Bertha's pride is held up to scorn and obloquy because she, who had been trained a princess, could not reconcile herself at once to be a peasant's child; and all romance takes for granted that the primitive instincts in every noble nature predominate absolutely and without a struggle over every mere social consideration. Miss Austen, who is never led away by what is not true, ventures, in opposition to this notion, to make one of her purest and most conscientious characters, Fanny Price, acutely ashamed of her father and of her home, because, under the circumstances, it was not possible for her to be otherwise. But, in Sir Walter Scott, romance predominates; and in the only example of false shame that occurs to us in his writings, Sir Piercie Shafton, a not unnatural sensitiveness is rendered extremely ridiculous. Modern writers enter into the sensation analytically, as they do into other complex workings of our social being. As we said at the outset, false shame and mere sensitiveness are closely allied. People make their way in the world a good deal better without either; and the one slips into the other so easily upon trying occasions, that it is wise not to test our friends too hardly, nor to expose them to the minor miseries and real dangers of this mood by anything in ourselves that may be rightly avoided.

FLUENCY.

THE present system of bringing different classes into friendly relations with each other through the medium of gratuitous instruction has, among its many excellent points, one which we regard as questionable. It cultivates fluency of speech and furnishes a school for ready utterance. The young member, the young squire, the young master, is encouraged to address his inferiors on matters that will inform and interest them, but on the understanding that he is to be superficial, — that he must not bring his mind to bear on the subject lest he should become deep and recondite, and so talk over the heads of his simple, ignorant hearers. His aim must be to say the commonplaces of his theme with facility, which is supposed to be the only gift such people can understand. All this our young orator is very willing to do. Whether aware of it or not, it is quite easy to him not to be deep, all he knows of his subject being its commonplaces; but, thus instructed, he has no fear of being shallow, and, even where consciously most weak, he believes he is only adapting himself to his hearers. So, strong in his condescension, he gets along to his own wonder and his friends' admiration, in a little flood of verbiage. It is, indeed, astonishing what a volubility, what a grand stream of words obedient to grammatical rules, a man can attain to if he only have sufficient contempt for his audience; and what gratification he derives from the exercise of this power of empty fluency and strictly verbal readiness. If he had respected his hearers, if he had been solicitous to give them the flower of his thoughts, and to put these into words which should recommend them to discriminating minds, if he had aimed at rigorous accuracy, feeling that there were listeners who could detect a fallacy and miss a link in the argument, he would probably have gone home humble and dissatisfied, with a sense of failure, conscious of many a pause and stumble and awkwardness of expression. But now he is complacent, and ready to begin again; for, after all, it is how we have said our say, rather than the force and merit of what we have said, which impresses us. It is how he has acquitted himself, what figure he has made, which dwells on the speaker's mind, and encourages or depresses him. And facility, of all things, gives this confidence.

There are, we suppose, many listeners who take the same view of facility, who are satisfied with it as a thing in itself, and believe it to be power and rhetoric, and an evidence of an absolute command of a subject. The least discriminating of any crowd will clap him most who says most words in a breath, if those words are said with sufficient confidence; but the admiration is by no means universal. Indeed, we suspect that, to a good many, fluency is irritating; so that, whenever we hear a man's rapid flow of words much talked of, we may be pretty sure, whether the commender know it or not, that he has felt it to be a bore. It is all very well to be carried away occasionally by a torrent of eloquence on some subject on which we feel that, but for some natural hinderances, we could be eloquent too; but even where thought and speech run together, as they do in the true orator, it is fatiguing to have to follow at a pace which is not our natural rate of thinking; and all we hear of hanging on the lips of speakers of this rushing, impetuous sort, means less than it says. Those who literally follow the processes of another mind have a task, whether a pleasant one or not; most persons are content with conclusions, and with any rapid, agreeable arrangement of words by which conclusions are arrived at.

It is amusing to hear how thinkers by profession

often regard this volubility, which takes simpler people as so fine a thing. When Madame de Staël visited Germany, the great minds there shuddered at the mere approach of this impersonation of "French volubility." Her inconceivable facility, her capacity of talking with freedom and fluency on every subject, simply annoyed and disgusted Goethe, who hated being put out of his way; and the more amiable Schiller, who pronounces her "of all living creatures the most vivacious, the most ready for argument, the most fertile in words," while he owns her to be the most cultivated and intellectual of women, yet groans over the "weary hours he has to pass" in her company, and attributes the interruption of her presence to the reverse of Divine influence. He was worried by the disturbance to his own trains of thought by her self-absorbed eloquence; while it is instructive to observe how the opposite circumstance on his side — his necessary shortcomings in the conversational duet — won and propitiated her. He spoke French badly; and when she perceived so many fine ideas struggling through oral difficulties, when she found him so modest and careless of personal success in his advocacy of his own views, she "vows towards him from that moment a friendship full of admiration." And is not this quite natural? His self-love had been wounded by the fearless readiness of her tongue; her tenderness had been roused by hesitations and failures which might be taken as a sort of homage to her own surpassing powers. There are, no doubt, times when a man may be as fluent as he likes, when the opportunity is his own, and he has prepared for it, — as a statesman on some great occasion, a lawyer who must seem to have impregnated his mind with his cause, and, perhaps especially, a preacher; though even here we feel that a momentary pause, an instant devoted to a choice of words, is a very becoming act of deference to an intelligent audience. But fluency, where we stand on equal terms with the speaker, has often some tinge of positive offence in it. He evidently thinks we can be amused and occupied at too easy a rate; and in the case we contemplated at starting, — the young orator condescending to his audience, — this state of things is soon reached. We should have liked him better if he had betrayed some timidity in our presence. We should have felt the thing less cut and dried if the ideas had had to struggle into fit words. We should not have been so utterly hopeless of his success in the field he was entering upon if he had seemed to realize its difficulties.

There is, however, a social side of the question, which is perhaps its more important one. Public fluency may have its drawbacks, and may go for very little; but, at any rate, it saves those who have to listen to such efforts the pain that comes with the opposite, and more dreaded, and more common defect, — an utter want of words. It is a sort of fluency familiar in private life which is most to be deprecated, a facility of speech which has grown out of certain causes, such as want of taste, ignorance of the meaning and force of words, and a habit of thinking in phrases, and talking for talking's sake. This is a habit encouraged and fostered by that want of respect for the listener which lies at the bottom, we verily believe, of all irritating forms of volubility, — the notion that something less than our best will do well enough for the person we are talking to, and, more than that, will amuse and gratify him. People with hobbies are always fluent, and we may say always wearisome; but they do not come under the present head, because their volubility is undesigned and spontaneous, and arises out of enthusiasm for their subject. They sin through egotism and defective sympathy, but not by condescension or disrespect. The quality we mean is acquired by practice, and is highly valued by its possessors, but is always based on some fallacy or insincerity. Either the speaker assumes to know more than he does, or to be more in earnest than he is; and the offence lies in the assumption that he can amuse without being amused, and can hold our attention while his own is preoccupied. It takes the whole mind to do anything well, but this fluency is effected by machinery and not by hand, and is, in fact, the knack of rapid talking and slow thinking.

So much talking with no heart in it has necessarily to be done that it may seem hard to be critical. Indeed, the cases that most readily occur of this volubility are in persons of great apparent kindness and good-nature, who perhaps, through a concurrence of circumstances, added to a naturally defective discernment, have fallen into it. Yet not the less is there a sense of condescension at bottom, which, if they could have suppressed it, would have saved them from a snare. The most excusable, and yet least excused, sort of volubility is to be found in women whose lot it has been to feel themselves the lively and invigorating spirit of their own small circle. Many a daughter, for instance, has learned to be garrulous, while she prided herself on her fluency, in her efforts to amuse her old parents. It seems cruel to pick holes in virtue like this, but the fact remains that she has acquired a terrible, rolling, flowing, amplified vocabulary, and that she is impressed with the notion that this ready tongue amuses and interests. And whence comes this but from the lifelong mistake that the elders on whom she lavished her efforts were really entertained by talk spoken, not because it was worth speaking, or because it expressed her mind and heart, but because she conceived it to be adapted to failing powers and the dull monotony of a secluded life? Yet all the while, no doubt, the old folks had constantly felt weary of the tongue that never ceased, and had kept quite unimpaired their ideas of what was really entertaining and worth saying and hearing. Trifles swelled into an unnatural importance, with all their details, are only amusing if the narrative occupies the narrator, and develops what is in him. It is impossible really to impart pleasure through conversation without sharing it; but the people we mean do not see this. There is the notion of conferring kindness, of dispensing a sort of intellectual alms out of the store of their indisputable superiority, which keeps them above the level of their hearers, and tends to make their conversation continuous, easy, unembarrassed, and rapid beyond any other system of talk under the sun. Invalids as well as old people must be very liable to the infliction of this patronage. We ought to be lenient to any form of testiness in them when we are conscious of having been talking in a groove, our thoughts not keeping pace with our words; for we should remember that any one who sits down expecting to entertain, without the further effort of rousing his powers to sympathy, is engaged in an act of presumption.

But this facility grows out of less amiable forms of self-conceit. The superiority of health over sickness, of spirits over depression, of vigor over decay, is patent and incontestable even to the suffering side; but there are people who are actuated in all they do and say, and in their way of doing it, by this same notion of conferring something, of being the obliging party, who practically forget that human beings stand in mutual relations. Education, if it does not immediately infuse these ideas, fosters them on the one hand, as it moderates them on the other. Thus a public-school training violently opposes any such inborn tendency, while certain private crotchety systems as actively develop it. All plans that put into children's heads the notion that it is their part to instruct or to patronize their elders, lay the foundations of a mechanical facility of speech, so that many would say that private education makes the best talkers. Young people who live at home, who perhaps are secluded from the amusements of their own age, and consequently from its society, are often indemnified for the privation by a notion carefully instilled into them of their usefulness. If they may not be amused after the careless fashion of their fellows, they can, at any rate, lay themselves out to amuse, and study to devote their talents to the service of others. This sounds excellent, but neither a good manner nor a good style is formed by it, because it is not the natural order of things. Young people ought to do one another good, and they ought to expect to get good from their betters, of whom they are the unconscious cheerers. But as soon as it formally enters into the mind of boy or girl to entertain their elders by their conversation, and to cultivate topics with this view, — as soon as they set themselves to talk as a sort of practice, collecting things to say, and storing them in their memory, not because they naturally interest them, but because they esteem them the sort of things for Mr. and Mrs. So-and-so, — they are laying the foundation of a facile, monotonous, inexpressive diction, which will haunt them through life. It will get them many a compliment, no doubt, and many a pretty speech of thanks, but will act as an insuperable impediment to all natural, free, enjoyable, and really profitable interchange of thought. A seed of conceit and self-estimation is sown which, because it is never recognized as a fault, or, rather, has all along been classed among the virtues, is scarcely likely to be eradicated. As we review all the fluent, complacent, mechanical utterances within our experience, certainly a sense of superiority, a mission to teach, to amuse, to do everybody good, or pleasure, lies at the bottom of them all. We find no recognition of mutual profit and service.

There is a volubility which is free from this charge. Children chatter, and some women chatter upon occasion; nay, men will now and then bubble over with words, and we like them all the better for it. It is an effervescence of the spirits, and if only the brain, by ever so trivial an exercise of its functions, has gone along with the tongue, the performance may be not only endurable, but delightful and exhilarating. But, if delightful, it is so because it is spontaneous, and indulged in for the speaker's own pleasure and need of sympathy, his hearer's benefit being the very last thing thought of. Alas both for those that speak and us that hear, if they ever come to value themselves upon this charming vivacity, and keep it up deliberately for our entertainment after their own is spent! But it may be said that we often have to talk for mere talking's sake, which is very true; and what philosophers have advised about never opening our mouths unless we have something to say is impracticable nonsense; but in this case we ought to take the necessity quietly, and as a condition of which each party is fully aware. The people we mean throw themselves into the situation with a spurious, unnatural relish, and use it as a sort of practice-ground for their powers. A half-hour of quiet dulness with a neighbor leaves us where it found us; but when one of the two throws himself with a false enthusiasm into the gap, and gets up a flow about nothing, — the words being always half a sentence, if not a whole one, ahead of the ideas, while still the sentences are neat and complete in their structure, and not a pin's point to be got in between them, — we come away with a sense of loss, and with a respect for the old science of humming and ha-ing which puts us out of humor with eloquence, — as though we had been shown the wrong side of it, — until our nerves and our memory have forgotten the infliction.

Contempt.

THERE is a good deal in the tone and manners of our day to foster a habit of quiet, passive contempt. In simpler states of society, the man who values himself highly has little scruple in confessing as much. Savages have no more reticence in parading their good points than peacocks. We know that even the Anglo-Saxon, when removed from the restraints of refined cultivation, can expatiate on his own merits with perfectly unqualified, unblushing complacency. American writers themselves are the first to acknowledge this as a characteristic of their remote outlying social life. There, men extol themselves in all the simplicity of an ignorance which knows nothing higher or better, and are frankly astonished at their own successes. Nobody is thought the worse of for praising himself; and where this is the case, whether in England or in the backwoods, we shall not find the practice out of favor or out of date.

But among ourselves it is out of date. A man cannot puff himself off with impunity, — without, in fact, being taken for a fool; and therefore, if he have ordinary capacity, he keeps within bounds. But not the less must the thought of the heart find some outlet. Men draw wide distinctions between pride and vanity, but both have at least this in common, they like to feel and to be acknowledged *first;* and both agree, not only in the craving for pre-eminence, but in the instinct to gain their end by a side-wind, — to boast themselves by implication, if circumstances will not permit the more agreeable incense of positive praise and adulation. This resource evidently lies in detraction, not spoken, not even conscious detraction, but a process of disparagement, by which, without any visible, active self-exaltation, the mind may keep uppermost in its own estimation. It is not possible, Clarendon observes, to overvalue ourselves without undervaluing our neighbors, — which he calls contempt. Contempt, then, in some form, is the necessary accompaniment of self-conceit. This is self-evident on reflection, though not always apparent. A man may be vain without being in manner contemptuous, and may indulge in a habit of general contempt towards others, when we do not think of him in connection with either pride or vanity. Nor is he necessarily vain for himself. A vicarious vanity belongs to all hero-worship. All people who have an idol are contemptuous; it is, indeed, a necessary part of their *cultus*. In either case, a man may be very far gone in contempt without being conscious of it himself, or committing any strong overt act offensive to the people about him; for, in its passive state, it is a mere practice of depreciation, and is taken for sensitiveness or a fastidious taste.

It is only now and then that a glimpse into motives discovers to us how much contempt there is in the world. We may live in intimate relations with people and only casually discover it. We may be acquainted with two sets, and some chance may first make us aware of the contempt in which each holds the other. Indeed, there is this poetical justice to console the observer, — the sentiment is seldom all on one side. We are sometimes taken by surprise at the amount of scorn and superciliousness which lurks under the most demure and seemingly unpretending exterior. It would not be comfortable to the most philosophical of us to know the tone of disparagement with which we are treated — the estimate at which our pretensions are rated — in certain quarters; and yet, if contempt is so common a habit of thought, all must fall more or less under it. There are natures with which we infallibly come in collision, so that they are driven in a certain self-defence to look upon our weak points, and take their stand upon them. We are told "not to take heed to all words that are spoken, lest we hear our servant curse us." We suspect that what is sometimes loftily spoken of as "withering scorn" is the "curse" here intended, especially as it is taken for granted that we likewise oftentimes curse others, and few persons' consciences can be quite clear on the point before us.

There are minds, belonging to respectable good sort of people too, so eaten into by this exclusiveness that they do not, at the bottom of their hearts, attribute to nine tenths of the people with whom they come in casual contact the same nature as themselves, the same affections and passions. It needs to be admitted to the honor of their friendship and esteem to possess either head or heart. A great deal that passes for goodness and even self-denial in the world has this passive form of contempt at its root. There is a tacit assumption that nothing good can be got out of people not included in a certain circle, sect, or party, — that of course their pursuits are frivolous, their aims mean, their conversation empty, their interests unworthy. Under a profession of humility, there is the notion that in intercourse all the gain and benefit must necessarily be on one, that is, on their side, — that they must impart all, and can hope to receive nothing good. This is the state of mind engendered by every form of exclusiveness, whether religious or social. It indefinitely restricts those natural bounds by which all intercourse must be ordered and limited. It is often called fastidiousness, but in fact the poor have as much of it as their betters, and decent people contract habits of sour seclusion from the same persuasion that their own company is the only safe company they can indulge in. There are persons of every rank who, as a matter of course, have a contempt for all people they do not know; just as the Dodson family despised all who were not Dodsons. They have fallen into a habit of regarding themselves as fountains of honor. To be out of their range is to be "these people" and "those people," the "good folks," the "wiseacres," the "gossips" of their neighborhood. It is amazing the narrowness, the dulness, the utter vacuity which can gather self-consequence and feed its importance by this contumelious mode of grouping and classifying the world outside itself; and yet, in a modified degree, this must be recognized as so common a habit of mind that we are convinced there is no rarer, as there is no more amiable and candid quality, than habitual justice to the motives of people not in our own set, and not subject to our influences.

Contempt may well be a common failing, for it is the easiest and most attainable form of self-assertion.

If we seek for instances, we are perhaps driven to witty or weighty examples, because such contemners can give a poignancy and force to the expression of their sentiments. We think of Gray pronouncing his own University, where he chose to spend his days, "a joy of wild asses," — or of Johnson, in dispute with an antagonist whom he considered beneath him, "withdrawing his attention to think of Tom Thumb," — or of Pope's "dunces" and "fools," or Warburton's "wretches" and "crews of scoundrels"; but, in fact, contempt can exist as vigorously without the pretence of brilliant and intoxicating qualities. Mr. Gedge, the landlord of the Royal Oak, could pronounce all the people he knew, "big and little, a poor lot," — could "say it often, and say it again," without being ever compelled to prove his own superiority to the people he despised. It was enough that he had an ideal. Indeed, as contempt is avowedly an act of opinion and judgment, it often flourishes most where there is no chance of being challenged to do better, and so of shaming the ideal. Beggars are proverbially proud, for this very reason, — they have an ideal for every station and every duty of civilized life, and are never called on to act out one of them. In the same way negroes are represented as supercilious. They have no social *status* apart from their masters. A white skin, then, is their ideal; they are contemptuous on quadroons as being "neither white *nor* black," — mere pretenders, as it were. It may be noted that nobody is so critical of dinners as the man that never gives them. With what weight he comes down on *entrées* and wines! How pure and fastidious his ideal on every point of order and arrangement! There is consolation, no doubt, in criticism of this character; for the time it equalizes distinctions. Our mind is above our fortunes. It is a great thing to know what is what, — to be on a level with the man we despise, if not even above him for the time being. What a solace to despair would poor discarded Brummel find, for the instant, in reducing his lost ally the Regent to the mere impersonation of obesity, — "Who is your fat friend?" The death of rich or great men often awakes the same sort of feeling. For once the living dog is master of the position and enjoys a triumph. When the young blood announced at his coffee-house the demise of the Grand Monarque, "So the old prig is dead at last," the airy familiarity was veiled contempt. He was inflated with more than a sense of equality. Death had placed him uppermost.

We have taken this side of our subject first, and regarded contempt in its passive and least intelligent aspect, because certainly learning, study of character, and mixing with mankind tend to allay and moderate it; but no doubt contempt is quite at home in its more recognized sphere, when backed and prompted by acknowledged superiority, and with seeming right on its side. It would not be easy to match from any age of the world, or any station of society, learned or ignorant, Mr. Ruskin's habitual contempt for all persons and things that contradict his views. It is headlong, monstrous, scarcely reconcilable with the possession of reason, and yet Mr. Ruskin has a wide knowledge of his own peculiar subjects, and might have been in his own line a great authority. But then he has acted on the assumption that success in one pursuit qualifies him to judge of all pursuits and all lines of thought. He has thought that study of art, of Turner's pictures, of nature, constituted him a judge, as well of all painters, as of every human need, character, and action. The conclusion he appears to have come to is, that the man who does not see all things with his eyes is wicked and stupid, a liar and a fool. This is contempt in its most rabid form. Thus, though his knowledge is great, it is ignorance which has misled him into the frenzies which we regret; and we think all misplaced contempt is to be traced to the same cause, — partial ignorance. Few recognized pursuits amongst men will cause contempt if we give ourselves the trouble to consider them attentively. But this clever men intent on their one hobby are as little ready to do as the most circumscribed intellect. All have some vein of Touchstone in them. When they survey something not in their way, in another world than theirs, they are ready to plume themselves on their want of sympathy as a sort of distinction, and to find it "meat and drink to see a fool." Thus severely practical minds enjoy their contempt for every effort of imagination. People who cannot see a joke have a contempt for fun. We have heard an artist merrily enlarge on the utter folly of the study of language. Swift condensed all that can be thought and said about music into the difference between tweedle-dum and tweedle-dee. Addison treats as a sort of drivelling the minute researches of the naturalist. Fifty years ago, half the world was contemptuous on science, and vast numbers now despise classical learning, as if it were a very clever and original thing to despise it. In one and all these instances we feel that only knowledge is wanting for the feeling to evaporate. There is one motive for contempt, however, on which the dull have it all their own way. There are people who not only despise any given form or pursuit of the intellect as perhaps we all do, but who have a contempt for active thought and all its results as such, — as if it were an inferior thing to write books, to know things, to think at all. They regard themselves as the Hindoos do their Supreme God, — as something above the vulgar processes of thought and action.

> "The learned is happy nature to explore,
> The fool is happy that he knows no more."

Analyzed, studied, looked in the face, it becomes a wonder that contempt should be so potent a thing as it is. The poet tells us that

> "He who feels contempt
> For any living thing, hath faculties
> Which he has never used; that thought with him
> Is in its infancy."

We ought, then, to despise the contemner as betraying defect and deficiency in the very act. But in truth it is an effort of independence which few can reach, to disregard the *dictum* of what seems deliberate weighty disparagement from any quarter whatever. Certainly there is a contempt justly terrible. The most confident and defiant would shrink from such scorn as Dante, in the very sublime of contempt, bestowed, for all comment, on the weak and pusillanimous band who had lived only for themselves: —

> "Non ragioniam di lor, ma guarda e passa."

But it is neither the contempt of goodness nor of intellect which men most dread. It is when it is vague, undefinable, neither to be got at nor propitiated, a mere fear and shadow, that it is the greatest bugbear, — the contempt of society or of the world for something, we know not what, and expressed or entertained by people whom, in their individual separate capacity, we may really rather look down upon. The sort of fear people are prone to have of servants illustrates, while it is an evidence of, this dependent and abject state of mind. Now, as servants are our fellow-mortals, they may be as worthy of the distinction of our fear as any one else; but the proverbial dread of falling in the opinion of a butler and incurring his contempt has nothing whatever to do with the great doctrine of inherent equality. It is the sneaking part of a man that here suffers, that quails under the notion that something is done to him which he can never know, from which there is no appeal. It is the closed doors of the servants' hall that invest the voice of opinion there in such terrors. Still, it has its grounds, and the very fear may work out its fulfilment. In externals, servants are very likely to be correct judges. They have an instinct as to who has lived in habits of command. They respect those who show by some nameless freemasonry that they are used to be attended upon, that the service of inferiors is part of their heritage. They have a nice though unconscious discernment of self-respect, and know at once where it resides. They like a man who asserts himself without bluster or assumption, they are judges of the particular qualities which affect their intercourse. To be afraid of a butler is, then, to have a misgiving whether we are quite the thing. The man who fears such contempt should take home the humiliating lesson, and regard it as a revelation of something wanting in himself. And so of all contempt, — either it is deserved or it is not. There is a remedy in either case, though we admit that our feelings cannot really be settled by square and rule as easily as this argument seems to imply.

No doubt, contempt has its charm where it procures a monopoly of regard. But this is but a narrow, ignoble satisfaction. A man much engaged in important concerns, who has to act with a variety of characters, tempers, and to clash with none, must not be contemptuous. If he have disdain in his disposition, he must suppress it at whatever effort. But what an advantage over others he has who, by nature or from an enlarged interest in human affairs, from caring for what others care for, is actually free from it, and can put himself in the place of the people he acts with frankly and unaffectedly! He finds a common ground in the midst of all differences of training or station, and thus feels the social link which it is the work of contempt at once to ignore and to break.

Dulness as a Sensation.

THERE are few things which show a more candid mind than a frank confession of dulness. It is an admission of occasional vacuity, of self-insufficiency, which very few can bring themselves to make, and which, when made, is not always received with the humanity and tenderness such ingenuousness deserves. People who never feel weary of their own company have a contempt for those who do, and often a very ill-founded contempt; for, in the first place, the difference may be one only of circumstances, — some people are much more exposed to dulness than others; and, in the next, satisfaction with our own company is wise or foolish according to the grounds on which it is founded. To be ever dull is, no doubt, a mark of human infirmity. For this exquisite mechanism of mind, thought, intelligence, ever to collapse, to lose spring and vigor, to suffer cold obstruction, should be a check to our pride of reason. But it is only felt to be so when our solitude is thus visited. To profess one's self dull in society where others are amused is a piece of pretension, a sort of boast, as implying a tacit superiority. But, in fact, this too argues deficiency and absence of power, often as great as the other. True vigor of mind and body is never dull, and can turn all painless conditions of being to an element of delight. If people are prone to feel dull, the scene of their dulness is more an affair of temperament, or at most of training, than of intellect.

We need not explain that the dulness we speak of is not any inherent quality of the mind, but a matter of feeling. It indeed implies a certain quickness of apprehension always to know when we are dull. There are existences so void of interesting, elevating, or inspiring circumstances, that only a dull head and a dull heart could reconcile themselves to them; but the leaders of such lives make them what they are, would not change them if they could, are content with them, and value themselves on that content. Supposed immunity from dulness, then, may proceed from all sorts of causes, creditable or the reverse. It may arise from activity of mind, fulness of thought, an uninterrupted stream of occupation, — which is always the assumed cause, — or from slowness, apathy, and a dead sterile imagination. Thus, a man may never be dull because he contains everything within himself, or because his heavy intelligence is on an exact level with his monotonous existence. Certain it is that there are many who avow themselves perfectly satisfied with their own company whose company gives others very little satisfaction, — who, if they are not dull, for anything we can see ought to be. It is an extremely happy thing in such cases that there is this just balance; for the fact is, it is only very lively or engaging people who can own themselves dull with impunity, — who can find sympathy, or even toleration, for their infirmity; and this for the obvious reason that in their case alone society is the gainer by it. Persons who are dull in both senses of the word at once are just the heaviest load social life can be burdened with. But charming people are the more charming because they are not independent of their fellow-creatures, — cannot pretend to the pride of seclusion, — and are thus driven, as well as led by their nature to show their best, conscious of some hidden, far-off bugbear, which haunts the long hours of uncongenial solitude, brightening the social scene by the contrast of its gloom. No doubt much may be done by practice and self-discipline to overcome this weakness, and every one, if he is wise, will struggle against it. But there is, all the same, an inherent difference between man and man which no effort can do away, and the man who wants companionship will always stand in a different relation to the world from the man who is independent of it. What we argue is, that it may be incompleteness, not inferiority: for, wherever the affections predominate, men will be dull when they cannot exercise them; and wherever the mind and intellect are worked by fits and starts, as some people are obliged to work them, — effort alternating with the indolence of reaction, — these intervals will be subject to conscious dulness.

We use the word dulness because our language has no other, but it is a vast deal easier to feel dull than to know what dulness is so far as to define it. Our classical writers all treat dulness as a quality. Men are dull, and are loathed by the wits accordingly. We do not for a moment assume any of our readers to *be* dull, — it is as much as we dare suppose, in this active-minded age, that any of them even *feel* dull under the ignominious condition of not being absolutely all in all, each to himself. Johnson recognizes the word in our sense, but he is obliged to depart from his rule and furnish his own example: — "Dull," "not exhilarating, not delightful; as, *to make dictionaries is* dull *work.*" But this does not get at the bottom of the thing. Dull work, dull leisure, dull company, dull solitude, — what is the common element in them all? Theologians tell us that our nature shrinks from absolute disembodiment, — that the spiritual part of us recoils from the idea of bare exposure of its essence, of being turned into space shivering, houseless, homeless. If we analyze dulness, there is something of this recoil about it. It is not otherwise easy to understand the horror with which men look forward to a threatened period of simple dulness. The protests, lamentations, self-pity expended on a brief season of dulness are called morbid, wrong, ridiculous, by the people who say they are never dull. The feeling expressed is so utterly incommensurate with the occasion, — taking into account the absence of positive pain, and the brief duration of whatever suffering there is, — that the whole thing is to them affected, unreal, preposterous. It is as if, like fretful children, these clamorers wanted something to cry for; and certainly, if it only meant not being diverted or exhilarated; dulness would be a weak subject of dread. But it is more. There is a foretaste, a threatening, of something worse, a touch of undefined spiritual terrors in all dulness. A day of simple vacuity, of not being amused, has no analogy with the dulness our active imagination realizes. Everybody is now and then neither doing anything, nor wanting to do anything, — unamused, and not wanting to be amused. Everybody is vacant sometimes, and does not dislike the sensation; but what has all this to do with dulness? A man is dull, it may be, to other people, but not dull to himself. Wordsworth prefers this state far before what he calls personal talk, — that is, gossip, — the relaxation of half the world.

> "Better than such discourse doth silence long,
>   Long barren silence, square with my desire;
> To sit without emotion, hope, or aim,
>   In the loved presence of my cottage fire,
> And listen to the flapping of the flame,
>   Or kettle chirping its faint under-song."

This is a picture of comfort, this is being at home with our household gods about us. Here the lazy, unoccupied spirit misses nothing. When people feel dull, there is a sense of deprivation and exposure. We are without something that answers to the mind for what clothing and shelter are to the body. We are weak, open to aggression; we have lost something; our completeness, our organization is affected. Time ceases to flow in this state, and prolongs itself into an uncertain sort of eternity which we are incapable of measuring. Immersed in dulness, even the future is too far off to excite hope; for dulness has in its very nature a touch of perpetuity. If we find ourselves, for example, in for four hours' perfectly dull talk, from which there is no escape, what good does it do to say, It is only four hours, What are four hours compared to a lifetime? and so on. We are not in a state to estimate the difference. Life itself *will* end, and we accept this truth more readily than that these four hours will end, which nothing seems to shorten. Solitary dulness is, no doubt, a more awful and more mysterious infliction than social dulness can ever be, but the majority of mankind are not exposed to this extreme pressure on mind and nerve, — they are not thrown for long periods utterly upon themselves. Dulness comes to most of us in the form of uncongenial company and occupation. Whenever the mind suffers from a suspense of its voluntary processes too long, we are dull, as in protracted or mistimed instruction or amusement. We are dull in scenes which make demands on our interest and intelligence that we cannot meet. We are dull when our mind, or one side of our mind, is defenceless, has lost its usual and necessary support, whether that support be habit — a word in itself conveying all our meaning — or the intervention of fresh ideas from without, for the want of which a painful void is felt. We are dull, whether we miss the familiar scenes, faces, voices, views of things on which we are wont to lean, or are shut out from that current of external life and thought through which the mind derives its sustenance.

Habit, in a sense, is the great resource against dulness. If we live long enough, we are never dull in doing what we are accustomed to do, and hence arises the little sympathy that age often shows to youth in this matter. Youth has acquired no confirmed habits. It is not desirable that a boy should be content always to spend one day like another, — to find his book all-sufficient, or his work or play all-sufficient. His mind, if healthy, has a clamorous appetite for change. His resource is variety of occupation, acquirement, and amusement, it is never mere resting in himself. He is not doing the best for himself if he is not occasionally some trouble to his friends in finding him fitting change and diversion, troublesome like the kicking, struggling, vivacious baby in arms, which will not allow itself to be forgotten. But parents who are proud of this infantine restlessness are often little lenient to the sufferings of dulness at an older stage proceeding from precisely the same cause. Unquestionably it is very convenient to others, and in a degree a sign of strength in the boy himself, to be sufficient for his own amusement, to have contracted habits of some sort early; but those who play the most active and stirring part in the world — practical men, men of action — have needed variety in their youth, and have been dull without it, conspicuously and energetically dull, not "listless, yet restless," like the worn poet in the same case, but powerful to fill the abhorred void by some congenial solace.

But habit — the panacea, the refuge, the protector — is so entirely dependent on circumstances that there is no dulness so pitiable or so incurable as that which proceeds from the breaking-up of an accustomed course of life, the dulness which proceeds from change, whether self-chosen or inevitable. Poor Charles Lamb, always ingenuous, how frank is he in the confession of his own delusions on this point! he who fretted over his compulsory monotonous life of thirty-five years of work, defied the chains of habit, and proclaimed that "positively the best thing a man can do is nothing, and next to that, perhaps, good works," and had his wish of idleness granted to him. If any man, he certainly had a right to trust to his resources, with his wit, his fulness of thought, aptitude for study, and felicity of expression. But these only helped him to feel, and aided him in portraying, the sufferings of his desolate unhoused spirit. He had worked in the heart of London amid "familiar faces," and changed it for the country with only strangers about him. How finely he insults the rural green, the varying seasons, the summer sun himself, in the dulness of his new life! "We do not live a year in a year now, — the seasons pass with indifference, — spring cheers not, nor winter heightens our gloom; let the sullen nothing pass." "In dreams I am in Fleet Street, but I wake and cry to sleep again. What have I gained by health? Intolerable dulness. What by early hours and moderate meals? A total blank. O, never let the lying poets be believed who 'tice men from the cheerful haunts of streets, or think they mean it not of a country village." "I dread the prospect of summer, with his all-day-long days. No need of his assistance to make country places dull. With fire and candlelight I can dream myself in Holborn." Such dulness is but home-sickness, the languishing of a sensitive nature for its native air and the shelter of old associations.

Though we say that confessions of dulness seldom meet with sympathy, unless relieved by wit and humor, yet all artistic pictures of dulness make a deep impression. This was the point of Mde. D'Arblay's Memoirs. The frightful dulness and vacuity to which her life was suddenly reduced appalled and fascinated every reader; and those who heard Mr. Thackeray's lecture on George III. will not forget those evenings spent all alike in dancing three hours to one tune, and going supperless to bed. It would have been better for himself and for his sons if the poor King had realized that this was dull work; and there is a great deal of dulness in the world, not confined to courts, that passes for virtue and turns into habit, which it is well should be now and then exposed. A sense of dulness might thus become a spur stimulating to higher and better satisfactions. The world is too often unfeeling on this point, yet it needs only to enter into another's dulness to pity it. We have heard somewhere of the inhabitants of a country town who, in their own way, were never dull. They had found out one remedy, the more effectual because they had never conceived of any other, — one and all played cards. At length a stranger arrived among them who could not take a hand at whist, who did not, in fact, know one card from another. He had to confess his ignorance before a large company. The circle heard in silent amazement. At length his host, realizing the joyless blank, the utter dulness of such an existence, exclaimed in terms which alone could convey the intensity of his sympathy, "What, sir! not play at cards! The Lord help you!"

Mistakes in Life.

THERE is something wonderfully pathetic in the idea of mistakes in life, even before we have any distinct impression with whom the mistake lies. The very term is a tender reproach upon Fate, as though that power set men to choose blindfold in matters importing their lasting interests, and punished them for choosing wrong. Regrets and repinings upon what might have been if things had not happened just as they did happen, — if we had not done just what we did do, — are a very familiar resource of melancholy or ill-humor. And a very natural one; for who can tell the weighty consequences of even a trivial action, all that is bound up in the decisions we are every day called upon to make upon what appear insufficient grounds for a right judgment? Most people, looking back on their career, must be tempted to think their life would have been more successful and complete but for certain blunders which were slipt into most unconsciously, and without any view to their bearing. They imagine that differences then seemingly unimportant would have altered their whole course, and altered it, as they are disposed to think, materially for the better.

The subject is a very wide and vague one. If we choose, we may call history a series of mistakes; but dispassionately to note the mistakes of others, either in a past age or in our own, is merely one form of observation, and as such does not affect the mind as a personal question, or influence the character in a selfish direction. There are people who are always dwelling on their own mistakes, and the mistakes of others towards them; and as this form of regret commonly takes the line of having cheated ourselves, or having been cheated, out of some of the good things of this world — place and name, more money and more friends, everything involved in success in life — it is a question whether the theme is ever a very profitable one, even where a man rigidly confines himself to his own share of the blunder. But, in fact, no one can indulge in this turn of thought long without implicating friends, connections, and allies in the disgrace. It is disagreeable to dwell for long exclusively on our own follies. The mind irresistibly seeks for partners in a scrape, and men are so bound up in one another that it can always find them. It is certain that people apt with the phrases, "It was a great mistake," "I made a great mistake," cannot carry on the strain beyond the first confession without falling foul of their friends' dealing with them. To start with, they are perhaps conscious of failing in certain preliminary elements of success; yet it is but a sour sort of humility to point out defects in their education, though there may be truth in it. The human race is a race of mistake-makers. Education has never been free from mistakes, and probably very grave ones. If a man has been brought up with scrupulous care, he is the victim of theory. If he has had the chances of other boys, study of individual character has been wanting. In some degree or other his spirit has either been cowed by severity or spoilt by over-indulgence. If left to himself, he acquires desultory habits. If held to hard mental labor, imagination is sacrificed. If parents have a large promiscuous acquaintance, they entail on their son the task of exclusion. If they belong to a party, he starts one of a clique; if they avoid society for his sake, he enters life solitary, unsupported, and without the power to make friends; if they interfered in his choice of a calling, his inclination might not be sufficiently consulted; if they left him to choose, he was thrown prematurely upon a judgment unfit for the responsibility. No circumstances have ever been perfectly happy, no management has ever been entirely judicious ; no man's friends have in all respects acted wisely by him ; and in every training a hundred things have been ill done or fraught with danger. It is the facility of shifting off some of the burden and the blame of our worst mistakes that makes this habit the most spurious of all forms of repentance, and often a mere ungrateful sham of contrition. To see a man, poker in hand, on a wet day, dashing at the coals, and moodily counting up the world's mistakes against him, is neither a dignified nor an engaging spectacle ; and our sympathy flags, with the growing conviction that no man is an utter victim to the mistakes of others who has not an ineradicable propensity to make mistakes himself, and that people are constantly apt to attribute a state of things to one particular condition or mischance which, sooner or later, must have happened from some inherent weakness and openness to attack. There is, besides, the experience, which must in its degree be universal, that wishes and expectations by no means necessarily suggest the means to their attainment, and that in youth especially we have often very earnestly wanted a thing, and yet taken no steps, or just the wrong ones, to get it, vaguely expecting our desires to accomplish themselves, though our outer life and actions may even wilfully run counter to them.

That subtle discrepancy between thought and action which is to be observed in speculative, self-conscious characters, brings about some of the more recondite mistakes of life. They are caused by refusing to believe in the natural consequences of actions, — by not counting the cost. Thus an act of large and exceptional liberality often looks like a mistake, — not at the time, when we are dazzled by the air of self-sacrifice, but when we compare it with the rest of a man's course, and note its effect upon his character, which is the only test of the consistency of the motive originally at work. Something on the same principle, Machiavel called a single unsupported act of generosity in an unscrupulous scheme of policy a mere blunder, — noting the great mistake it is to "mingle isolated acts of mercy with extreme measures." It sounds horribly cold-blooded, and sinks him lower than ever in the disesteem of modern readers; but he may have taken a juster measure than we do at this distance of the motive which prompted the discordant generosity. However, we must not dwell on this part of our subject, though a writer in the "Spectator" did propose it "as no unacceptable piece of entertainment to the town to inquire into the hidden features of the blunders and mistakes of wise men."

Of course, all people reviewing their own lives

must see in them great mistakes, — wonderful mistakes, — perhaps a mere series of mistakes as compared to that ideal of life with which they started, and in contrast with which the reality is a thing of shreds and patches, beginnings without endings, ceaseless fluctuations of design, so that we have something to do to trace the one mind at work through the successions of change. Yet we may be sure that this is just what others can see in us. It may be noted that where men themselves attribute ill-success or mischance to separate distinct mistakes, — as, for instance, to the choice of such an adviser, the engaging in such a speculation, — those who have to observe them trace all to character. They see that if failure had not come at such a juncture, it must at some other, from certain flaws in the man's nature which he must heal and repair before he can go straight, — that mistakes simply mark occasions when he was tested. We see in a career a hundred chances thrown away and wasted, not at all from accident; though the actor, looking back, does not know why he chose the wrong, and is still only aware of having vacillated between two courses in a certain toss-up state of mind, in which, as far as he sees, he might just as well have chosen right, he being the last to remember that a crisis is the occasion for hidden faults and predominating influences to declare themselves, so that his mistakes were, in a manner, inevitable. For example, one man rushes headlong into an uncongenial, imprudent marriage, which may be considered *the* mistake, *par excellence*, of life. Can there be, properly, anything merely accidental in such a step? Does it not belong to a certain course of action, — to a vein of folly or conceit of which something of the sort is a natural sequence, which he only escapes by a happy accident or want of opportunity? Another man is intending to marry all his life, and dies a peevish old bachelor, owning his mistake; but others can trace a whole course of weak compliance, or selfish, ungenerous caution, as the cause of his present isolation.

It may be that the errors of a consistent, deliberate course of action only go by another name; but certainly the habit, in all its flagrancy, not only of making mistakes, but of moaning over them, belongs to those who act on impulse, and disdain a producible reason for their actions. This might seem self-evident; but not only are the people prone to impulse, incorrigibly proud of it as being akin in their mind to genius, which can afford to despise the slower processes of reason; but the world does much to foster the idea, by attaching high-sounding adjectives to the word, — so that good impulses, noble impulses, generous impulses, run off our tongue of themselves. Yet, in fact, the majority of impulses are not good or noble, and experience shows us that impulse is amongst the most inconvenient and questionable guides in human affairs. A good impulse either means an inspiration, or it is a good habit of mind, showing itself on some sudden call with a readiness of response which is mistaken for spontaneous resolve. But the impulse we see most of is the reverse of this, and proceeds from some looseness of mind which defies and forbids the formation of habits, which forms nothing, but drifts along, — when it acts on ordinary principles of conduct, — without acquiring any lasting impressions from custom, or any adhesiveness; so that, when a new or bizarre suggestion presents itself, it comes with the force of a command. Why not? why should n't they? — and there is no counteracting stay of habit to provide an answer, or stand against the delirious joy of novelty, — the gambler's excitement of putting the happiness of his future on a chance for the mere thrill of seeing it imperilled.

After all, we shall not often get the actor and the looker-on to be of the same mind as to what are mistakes. As the epicure lays the account of his indigestion to the few drops of cream in his after-dinner cup of tea, so the repiner over his own destiny sets his misfortunes down to trifling indiscretions, or even to what others might consider exceptional exhibitions of good sense; while the decisive failures, the incontrovertible mistakes, are defended to the death. Some of this school have only one mistake to reproach themselves with, but this recurring, as we are given to understand, at various turning-points of life, — that of not having taken their own way, but having allowed themselves, at some critical juncture, to follow the advice, the example, the opinion of others.

Persons of a speculative cast can scarcely escape this habit of mind. Their own experience is much like Mr. Clough's: —

> "How often sat I poring o'er
> My strange distorted youth,
> Seeking in vain in all my store
> One feeling based on truth";

for a certain intellectual activity prompts to a perpetual review and suspicion of the past. Authors, the picked men of this class, who are driven by their calling to utilize the actions and proceedings generally of so much of mankind as come in their way, may be said to constitute themselves *the* authority on all questions of cause and effect, and to pronounce *ex cathedrâ* on what are the mistakes of others; though their attitude of critics of the human race diverts them from personal vigilance, and makes them crying examples of mistakes in their own persons.

Thus we may see them very much alive to the world's mistakes towards them, and very blind to the real cause, often to the real facts, of their own. It is next to impossible but that writers, as a class, should be discontented men; for human nature craves for action, and, in the long-run, the observer, whatever his success in his own field, will feel it a mistake that he has not been an active worker instead of a chronicler and speculator on others' work. They are almost as certain, too, to overvalue their own judgment, and thus to lay the cause of their mischances at the wrong door. Thus the autobiographies and personal revelations of literary men represent them all as victims of mistakes.

But all people who are not men of action are not therefore men of thought. Mistakes are a very prolific subject with all who judge of things, as so many do, solely by the event. There are persons who live in the belief that they are wise till something happens wholly irrespective of their own conduct or motives, when they spring as suddenly to the conclusion that they have been fools. It is wonderful what steps will be regretted, — what natural, proper, nay, inevitable steps, — where the event does not vindicate a course of action. It is imperative on many tempers to blame somebody, — anybody, — when things do not go as they would have them. Thus a man meeting with a railway accident is bent on proving it a great mistake that he went by that train at all. The irrevocable, with all unreasoning natures, is forever prompting this illusory, deceitful form of self-blame, which issues in nothing, for it has not taught them any new principle of conduct.

Many people attribute to themselves a series of mistakes from a mere over-estimate of their powers. It is their only method of accounting to themselves why they were not where their deserts should place them. It is soothing to their vanity to lay their failure to the charge of some defect in policy or judgment. They are at the foot of the ladder instead of the top, and find a feeble, vapid consolation in counting up a series of isolated blunders. It all comes from not embracing that opening, from stopping short on the way to success a day too soon, from an ill choice of advisers at some important crisis, and so on. But the truth is, everybody is making such mistakes always. No man can get on without the power, not of avoiding mistakes, but of nullifying and mastering them when made. Yes! no doubt every life is full of mistakes, and it is a further argument against morbid dwelling upon them that we can rarely find in our own case which of them has told lastingly against us. Going by analogy, — observing what sort of mistakes press and gnaw on the minds of others, — our own sensitiveness is far from being an infallible judge. We may then be attaching mighty consequences to some indiscretion which has really served us well, while the mistake which has damaged us may lurk altogether out of our cognizance. Especially we may take for granted, of every man who sits and murmurs over the mistakes of others towards him, that, in fact, he is suffering infinitely more from the consequences of his own.

SCENES.

CONSIDERING how popular fiction is, and that it mainly depends for its charm on scenes, — that is, on humanity being exhibited in its more striking combinations, where the whole nature is stirred by emotion of some kind, — it is strange what a universal horror there is of a scene in real, actual life. The very idea of being exposed to one puts us under the apprehension of being made painfully ridiculous, of being taken possession of, and losing the guardianship of ourselves. Every one shares the dread. Amongst people who represent society, the recoil is unanimous. Of course, the alarm is greatest where something harrowing and distressing is apprehended, and this needs little accounting for; but mere pleasurable excitement, if it threatens their serenity, is a thing that well-to-do, comfortable people always eschew if they can. Now we suspect that men generally assume this reluctance to having their feelings meddled with to arise from the fact that something very startling, — some effect of roused emotion which should shake them to their centres, — would be the consequence of breaking through their crust of reserve. They take for granted they must be cold and self-restrained outwardly, because they have such a great deal of feeling at bottom, though kept religiously out of sight. There are people, for instance, who never will say good-by, or encounter a parting, because they cannot stand it. Now we do not want scenes to come into fashion, and should be sorry to see the world turn maudlin and sentimental; but still there is a view of this horror of scenes, and this extreme solicitude to avoid them, which seems to us more in accordance with probability than the one thus readily acquiesced in. Men imagine they are afraid of any expression of feeling because they might risk exposing themselves by some unmanly excess of vehement emotion; but have they not also other grounds for evading the trial? We greatly suspect that, under this superficial belief that we should be too deeply moved in certain situations, — perhaps torn and convulsed by tragic or pathetic passion, — there is a lurking, unacknowledged misgiving that possibly we should not be moved enough for our credit, or even for our self-esteem: for to discover that the crust is impenetrable, — in fact no crust at all, but just nether millstone inside and out, — would be by no means gratifying to our self-love. Yet people whose feelings are never reached, who carefully keep themselves out of the way of having them tried, are much more likely to have too little feeling than too much. And how many injustices and cruelties are committed, how many abuses go on, because of this dread of breaking the tranquil surface of things! And why this dread? Because there is a vague notion that people cannot bear — that they would sink under, or be permanently injured by — things which they could bear perfectly well, and which would not injure them at all. We are convinced that too much feeling, as a disinterested benevolent affection, is one of the very rarest excesses to be found in human nature. The purest feeling submits to the inevitable; and, when tinged with selfishness and obstinacy, it yields and calms itself, with whatever ill-grace, so soon as nothing is to be gained by holding out.

The majority of men, from the habit of indulging a selfish fear of pain and annoyance, have not feeling enough, — they would be ashamed of themselves if they knew how little. We are justified in saying this of any one who, when nature and the occasion demand some expression, makes no sign, — who is cold and forbidding when he ought to be warm and sympathizing. We cannot believe in any feeling that never shows itself; or, only on extreme occasions which disorganize the mind and will; though there is a romantic notion the reverse of this, connecting a stern impassive manner, under all ordinary trials, with hidden fires and a world of unexpressed passion if it could but be reached. It may be that peculiar circumstances will rouse the smouldering flame into a brief conflagration; we may see a struggle of half temper, half feeling, in these harder natures; but what good does it do, and why do we prize it because it is hard to reach? It is not fair to value pity or tenderness in proportion as they are unwillingly given; and yet how often it is so! "You have no heart there, my dear Fontenelle," said a witty Frenchwoman, laying her hand on the waistcoat of her friend, "it is another brain"; but if Fontenelle could have been betrayed under extreme pressure to exhibit some symptoms of humanity, there are many who would deem the emotion, when it came, all the choicer and more precious for its rarity; and so, probably, would the man himself, taking good care at the same time that the thing should never happen again.

But even where there is the average of heart and kindliness, how little cause is there for alarm on this head! How soon people get over things! Which of our acquaintance have we any reason to suppose has permanently suffered by his feelings? How rarely have we seen our friends deeply moved! And if we have on some trying occasion, what harm has it done them to sound for a while the hidden depths of their nature, and how long did the pressure last? We do not wish it otherwise. We are not complaining that passionate feeling is not lasting, — there would be no peace, no living, if it were; but we argue from it that the alarm about scenes is not really chargeable to any excess of sentiment in most of us. We are all made of pretty tough material, and can bear a good deal. In some the objection may no doubt be traced to a reasonable and dignified reluctance to having our more secret, subtle life intruded upon without urgent necessity. In the majority, it arises from that preference of the superficial over the deep, as involving little trouble and taking least out of us, which is amongst the most universal of human characteristics, and which leads us constantly to prefer the pleasure that costs us least effort, even while we know intenser enjoyment from the exercise of our nobler faculties to be within reach. In a great many, it is attributable to the opinion that affected, shallow natures revel in scenes, and therefore that manliness must keep clear of every expression of feeling. There are people, no doubt, the opposite of those we have hitherto discussed, who have a relish for excitement of the weeping, demonstrative, tragic sort, — people who, from natural fussiness and the want of good social training, love to display themselves in melodramatic action, and whose fancy is easily caught and tickled by sudden, and, as it seems to them, touching situations. While they are expressing as much real emotion as is in them, they are not insensible to an agreeable consciousness of doing the thing well and putting colder natures to shame. These persons, from thinking a good deal of themselves, and very likely of their family peculiarities, have less tact than their neighbors, and are apt to enlist unwilling recruits into the service of their gushing effusions; and they may well make scenes a term of horror and reproach to us all by getting them up with unsympathizing seconds, caught at unawares, who have to walk through their part in unspeakable quandary and confusion.

It is much the same spirit which enjoys these little emotional dramas that dictates the grand, pompous system of breaking evil tidings, which, ingeniously managed, is greater torture than the ill news itself, the operator all the while engrossed with his own share of the performance, and so profoundly impressed with his own neat exordium as to have no attention for its effect upon the sufferer. A person well up in the art of protracting an announcement may, in the course of his gradual disclosure, convey to a lively, excited imagination a taste of every conceivable calamity. Nothing comes up to what the fancy can conjure out of vague threatenings of evil; and the curious thing is, that people of this turn — and it is another mark of their total want of observation — will always fancy others so much more tender and susceptible than they can pretend to be themselves. Men who ought to be perfectly aware that, out of their own immediate domestic circle, — wife and children, and their pecuniary affairs, — there is nothing they could not face calmly, and, after an hour's thought and speculation upon it, feel perfectly used to as an old idea, will "break" the most natural intelligence to men whom they have no reason to think different from themselves. They will attribute to remote consanguinity a power over the affections which belongs only to our own hearth, and will keep a man on tenter-hooks in announcing, with circumlocution and a parade of precaution, the demise of a cousin or an uncle with whom he was never a very particular ally during life. The victim would exclaim, in peevish relief, "Is that all?" but that there is an instinct in the most random of us always alive to protect the credit of our feelings. Nobody likes to take things more coolly than is expected of him, — the delusion is winked at, — and his friend goes on his way with all that glow and effusion of sentiment men feel when engaged in their peculiar vocation.

The fact is, feeling is a mysterious thing about which all have a curiosity in their neighbor's case so long as it can be indulged without committing self. How a man will take an event which closely concerns him, is amongst the first speculations of the circle to which he belongs. The quickest observation, the keenest study of character, can never foretell how those we know best will be affected by any new or startling occurrence. A great many people never reason on their own sensations at all; experience does nothing to disturb a certain conventional standard of propriety. But this is not all. Feeling is, in fact, a capricious quality, subject to a hundred unaccountable influences, so that no degree of penetration can arrive at any certainty, or can settle what people will do or say under given contingencies, where the romance of real life is in action. People's dislike of scenes solely arises from the notion that they may be implicated. They are curious to hear of, and are even not unwilling to witness, human perturbations, where this apprehension does not come in; only the more educated and thoughtful persons are, the less they can contemplate the possibility of being unconcerned spectators on such occasions.

The poor are exceedingly subject to this hunger for witnessing the passions at work, as opposed to the reluctance we have dwelt upon in persons subject to the world's training; and they have this to be said for their curiosity, — that whereas education and society bend all minds to a certain external conformity, warning the cold against an unconcerned manner, and instilling the necessity of self-restraint on warmer temperaments, — in the humbler classes the real working of the mind is laid bare with little effort at disguise or assumption. Where the affections are strong and the temper ardent, all the stormy tumults of tragedy and the vehemence of passion are brought within the compass of our belief; but where the nature is dull, and further deadened by stolid ignorance and daily sordid cares and indulgences — till the present is all in all, and nothing can touch the mind that does not touch the senses — there is no decorous pretence, no propriety to stand instead of feeling. They do not know that anything is expected from them, either for their own credit or the common credit of humanity. They allow us to see all the nakedness of the land. An old couple lost their son in the late war, and it became the painful duty of their pastor to communicate the intelligence to them, which he did with all the cautious tenderness he could command. There was a pause, which the old man first broke as he turned to the bereaved mother, in safe reliance on her sympathy, with the words, "Now, we ought to get something by that." Every class has its selfish, unnatural fathers; but such simplicity of egotism can only be betrayed where the restraint of public opinion is unknown.

Considering the irksomeness of flighty, ill-timed exhibitions of feeling, which are annoying on one side and deteriorating on the other, we might well leave the subject to individual tastes and inclinations but for one consideration. The real grievance and mischief of dread of scenes lies, of course, in its interfering with expression of sympathy where sympathy is a positive need. When men are under the first pressure of real trouble, they are not afraid of scenes, — that is, as an ordinary rule, they are not. It is often the only comfort the occasion allows them. Some one to talk to, some eye that will pity, is then the first want; and even beyond this is the curious longing, which belongs to people in an unhinged state of feeling, to see in others some effect of the disorganization they are conscious of in themselves. They require some reflection of their own disorder, — they want to see their friend visibly altered and changed by participation with their trouble. They even run through the circle of their acquaintance with a vague curiosity how they will take what affects themselves so deeply. And in this hour of weakness, in this unconscious yearning for something new, some relief from the burden of importunate thought, the friend who dreads a scene stays at home, and argues with himself and others that he can do no good, — that is, he cannot restore the dead, or repair a broken fortune, or end suspense, or make an inconstant lover faithful, or reform a bad son. He knows he would be welcome, — this we take for granted; but because he can only sit and listen, and share the sorrow, and show a pitying countenance, — bring some change, some new suggestion, some fresh aspect of things, — he stays at home, avoids a scene, and adds a sense of disappointment and chill desertion to troubles which he might have helped his friend to bear, if not to escape from. After all, people generally lose more than they gain by avoiding anything painful that comes naturally in their way. No decent man can feel comfortable while in his heart he knows himself a coward. And, in other respects, those who exercise their feelings are happier than those who suppress them. They have more the sense of living; they are more at one with the great human family; they are occupied with the interests which have the strongest hold on others; and, above all, they have not cut themselves off from the study — of all others the most absorbing — of human nature. A real knowledge of character can only be acquired by seeing men under every variety of circumstance; and we have an imperfect, and very often false, idea of every man whom we only know at ease and entrenched behind all the restraints of society.

Acquaintances and Friends.

THERE is a very common confusion of ideas between acquaintances and friends, which not only gives false notions of society but results in a good deal of conceit and harsh judging. Some people are always wondering and regretting that acquaintances do not turn into friends by a sort of natural growth or transformation; while others affect to despise acquaintances, because they are not friends, and therefore not worth having. In talk and in theory, "mere" acquaintances, as they are called, are disparaged. Acquaintanceship is thought a worldly thing, and indeed there is no surer test of worldliness with a good many minds than that persons should accept society for what it is, — the intercourse of acquaintances, — and find pleasure in it. To know many people, and to know them mainly through their open and palpable qualities and gifts, — to like their company, without curiously inquiring whether the existing superficial sympathy may be forced into deeper and more intimate currents of feeling, — is supposed to imply a frivolous, a cold, or a worldly temper. This sentiment is embodied in so many representations of life, from that of the austere professor who denounces dinner-parties because the guests are apt to take an airy and cursory view of things, and to abstain from probing into each other's profounder convictions, — who would confine every social demonstration to tea-meetings of a very few friends of identical habits and feelings, — down to that of the toper who sings over his cups, "Only give him his friend and his glass, all the rest of the world may go hang," that it may be called universal. That is, it is universal as a sentiment, for it is incapable of being really put in practice. Everybody *has* acquaintances, could ill spare them, and is really greatly indebted to them, even though there may be no chance of the relation ever changing into that of intimate friendship. Persons are not worse than we are, because entire sympathy is incompatible between our natures and theirs. Yet, when people talk and write of acquaintances in contrast with friends, there is generally a growl at the hollow world, as though the grumbler stood outside of it. No such thing. The world may be hollow, but this is not a necessary proof of it. It is no sign of its hollowness that men who meet one another on certain understood terms of guarded approach do not get nearer. Our friends may be hollower, less sincere, than our acquaintances, and yet may suit us better, — may reach a different, deeper, more intimate part of us, adapt themselves with a nicer fit and adjustment to what is peculiar and characteristic in us, and be bound to us, and we to them, by a stronger, more exacting, and more sacred tie than acquaintances, however estimable.

It is clearly necessary to establish the generic difference between friendship and ordinary social intercourse before we can settle the claims and duties of each. Once grant that mere acquaintanceship is a good and profitable relation in itself, though developing into nothing closer and warmer, and we shall see that a great deal that has at all times been said on this subject is unjust as well as impracticable, through the neglect of proper distinctions. It is through our circle of acquaintance, so far as it is at once well chosen and extensive, that we realize our duties as citizens, so to say, — that we derive our knowledge of mankind, and learn the claims of our own class and what we owe to it, — that we acquire propriety of manner and independence of thought. Acquaintanceship is, in fact, the medium through which we see the world, by which we touch it and become cognizant of public opinion. If it were possible for men to have none but intimate friends between them and the vast system at work around them, they would degenerate into every form of crotchety eccentricity, overbearing tyranny, or enervating dependence. But it is quite clear that this external social connection, to be of mutual service, must be under quite different laws from those which regulate friendship; and this is just the distinction which prosy moralists, or moralists when they are prosy, have refused to acknowledge. From our childhood we have read denunciations of society as heartless and ungrateful for letting its members slip through, and pass out of sight, under the touch of misfortune. The popular, picturesque illustration of this in story-books used to be the easy, careless, amiable spendthrift, who, after lavishing his fortune upon so-called friends, was, in the evil hour, deserted by them. Now, friends are not the sort of people men do lavish fortunes upon. The spendthrift wished to make a figure or to enjoy himself, and collected about him whoever would further this end. But it was really the fault of the spender, not of the world, that he should drop through after his money was gone. The assumption was preposterous, that, after his own means were wasted, his acquaintance should make all straight by giving him theirs, — which was the moral apparently pressed on our raw and perplexed judgment. Acquaintances are not called upon to advise one another on their private affairs. They have not data upon which to judge of prudence or imprudence. On this point each man must take care of himself, and do his duty to society by setting a wise example. It is not really heartless to refuse to share our possessions with every man with whom we have interchanged dinners; and altered fortunes may act as a separating influence without any just charge of coldness on the more fortunate party, because there has always been a tacit understanding that the intercourse is subject to certain conditions. Towards acquaintance men act in their corporate capacity as members of society; while friendship is strictly a tie between two contracting parties, with which society has no right to interfere. Of course, people act upon this view of the difference between the two relations; but if they act under a confused idea that there is something insincere and heartless in it all the while, they are likely to *be* heartless and insincere. They shuffle, and shirk, and fail in the kindness and tenderness which belong alike to every form of intercourse. In fact, people are often unfeeling, and even cruel, to old acquaintances, because they fear that sacrifices which are only due to friendship will be expected from them.

If it were true that it is hard-hearted and hollow

not to hold by acquaintances through every turn of fortune, every change of circumstances, and every difficulty that time throws in the way, then the fewer of them we form the better; and some people, in argument at least, are quite ready to act upon this principle, and to confine their society to those whom, in an exact sense, they call friends. But in fact, in the true meaning of the word, people cannot have many friends; nor will they have any more for rejecting acquaintances, nor be any better morally; while intellectually they will miss a great freshening and polishing influence on human nature, which requires for its development popular and general intercourse, as well as particular intimacies. In defending society from the charge of being necessarily hollow, by showing that its ordinary intercourse is not founded on false pretences, we are not denying that it may be unsatisfactory. It is unsatisfactory that appearances do not go for all they seem to the uninitiated, that reality eludes men's grasp, that all people who reflect on their position find something illusory and infirm in their hold of things. Certain it is that there is no complaint more universal than the want of a staff of real friends. People cannot understand how, friendship being so human a thing, there should be so little of it. They perpetually attribute the defect in their own life to circumstances, and generally with a show of reason; and all that can be said is, that circumstances which seem so trivial, or so peculiar, or so accidental, appear to be in this matter a universal agent. The cry, after all, does not come from the affections. It springs from the desire to be a living, acting, necessary part of the world in which we find ourselves. Nobody really feels himself to be substantially what he seems. People who are called "in the world," and are looked upon by their distant friends as in the turmoil and heart of things, feel themselves excluded from the mystery and the secret of it all. The people they live and act with, and with whom they are identified as one — perhaps exclusive — community, show them only their outside. They stand loose from them; they never really touch; they are conscious of illusion and slipperiness, — of a sort of imposture. Those who have never felt the excitement of being part of what they see, of owning a place in the active social fabric, wonder how, in their sleepy circles, acquaintance does not grow into something warmer through the mere lapse of years, — how the solemn, dull, stated meetings should not, through mere friction and contact, kindle into something genial. Hopeless aspiration! for there is no greater impossibility than that a twenty years' guarded acquaintanceship should, under any conceivable circumstances, change into friendship, or even into active, unrestrained sociability.

This impatience and repining is natural in the young, whose hopes are alive and their anticipations all astir on every new acquaintance out of whom imagination can construct a castle or a vision. Until experience has done its work, there is something intolerable to ardent temperaments in facing the slight tenure which they really have on all they see, — the little hold they have, or are ever likely to have, on what they take society to be. To be attracted by people, to meet them at stated times, but always with some impediment to any effusion of thought and sentiment, — to make no way, — to find the same friendly cordiality always succeeded, when the occasion is past, by the same indifference, — disgusts them, and makes them rail, not, of course, at this particular instance, but at the society which permits such things, and holds congenial souls back from the thrilling pleasures of a real encounter. They are apt to think their elders cold, and spoilt by the world, who resign themselves to things as they find them, are less exacting from fate, and expect nothing from society but what it gives. They cannot understand persons who enjoy an agreeable acquaintance, though the periodical meetings lead to nothing further, and who learn to be satisfied with the refreshment and variety as far as they go, without expecting deeper satisfaction from such intercourse, or any fundamental changes in their daily life, — who can estimate pleasant people at their full value, yet reconcile themselves to the conviction that these people's choicer gifts and warmer intimacies are not for them. Time shows us all that a man may have much in him which suits us and fits in with us in matters of general interest, yet be wanting on all points necessary for private satisfaction. These public qualities are good and worthy ones, and it is fair that they should have their arena and be esteemed at their true value, though the same mind may have inferior or, to us, utterly uncongenial elements. Moreover, we learn by experience that there are real substantial good qualities which yet fit people rather for acquaintances than friends, because these qualities are constantly clogged with some alloy which tells upon close intimacy. Thus, brilliant conversational powers are inestimable in an acquaintance, but have certainly their drawback in a friend; and a good grasp of general subjects, or wit, or polish, or grace of manner, are compatible with particular intellectual wants and defective sympathies which might, and constantly do, detract from their charm and disqualify for friendship. Again, there is a diffusive benevolence and general good-nature, incapable of distinct preferences, but quickened into activity by cheerful scenes, which makes "nice" people and desirable acquaintances, though, for our part, we should not look to them in the emergencies of life. Indeed, a host of natural deficiencies may be kept out of sight in guarded intercourse, and we may be only gainers by what general society fosters and brings to light. So far, there is no "hollowness" nor worldliness in those who accept society for what it is, — a scene where all are on their good behavior, and in a position to show their more agreeable qualities and to keep the rest in the background. When people, through habit and deadness to higher things, grow satisfied and content with acquaintances only, and have lost even the yearning for anything deeper or more intimate, then, of course, they become open to the charge of hollowness. But this is not the occasion to talk of club windows, of Bond Street loungers, dowagers, old stagers, men about town, and professional diners-out, who in one sense know, hundreds, and in another have not a friend in the world; though many of these folks, whom the young, affluent in hope and inherited friends, contemn as heartless, used-up worldlings, are friendless, not from incapacity for friendship, but because none except acquaintances are left to them at a time when friends are not to be had for the wish. It is wonderful what one of these old fogies now and then turns into, — what heartiness he will develop when circumstances give him a chance; though we own the transformation is a rare one.

What we would say is, that acquaintances, and acquaintances only, can awaken certain feelings and do certain things for us. It is precisely because we do not know them intimately, nor they us, that this service is rendered. Society, as it is conducted in highly-civilized and artificial communities, requires great powers of reticence, selection, and self-control in those who mix in it. Inexperienced persons, on finding themselves suddenly part of it, are almost certain, if they throw themselves into the scene at all, to commit themselves by over-energy of expression, by too earnest a tone, by showing parts of themselves for which this is not the fitting sphere; and on becoming conscious of this difference between themselves and those around them, a sense of resentment is awakened against a state of things which has made their sincerity and warmth appear *outré*, and perhaps ridiculous. But the necessary repression of what it is delightful to impulsive natures to express is really a check upon vanity and display. Every person accustomed to society feels that he must not obtrude even his most heartfelt convictions too forcibly, where it cannot be done without also obtruding himself. The light, passing, superficial treatment of subjects even of interest in mixed circles does not imply, as some suppose, that people have not profound convictions which, elsewhere, and on what seem to them fitting occasions, they can express with both the force and warmth their importance demands. But experience has taught them that the republic of society will not and cannot stand dictators, and that the unrestrained liberty of speech of one would be the subjection and suppression of the rest. People may fancy themselves superior who will go nowhere where they may not speak their minds, and who shun all that are not of their own way of thinking. But they miss a discipline which might make them of service in their generation; and they also miss the taste of that exhilarating yet unselfish pleasure which minds open to the influence of society can alone experience through the genial contact of numbers, — "that pleasure the mind seasoned with humanity naturally feels in itself at the sight of a multitude of people who seem pleased with one another, and are partakers of the same common entertainment."

Saying Disagreeable Things.

SOME people, not otherwise ill-natured, are apt to season their conversation with disagreeable sayings, unpleasant comments, uncomfortable insinuations. Such a person, we sometimes hear, is a good sort of fellow, but he has a way of saying disagreeable things. Such a woman can be very charming when she pleases, but— In fact, these people are never spoken of for three consecutive sentences without a qualification. A disagreeable thing is distinguished from an impertinence, which it often closely resembles, by certain marks. In the first place, an impertinence we need not stand, but the other we often must, aware that it is the result of certain conditions of our friend's mind, which, as we cannot hope to alter, we must resign ourselves to. An impertinence may or may not be true, — its main design, independent of truth, is, more or less, to insult. It is of the essence of a disagreeable thing that it should be true, — true in itself, or true as representing the speaker's state of feeling. And yet an unpalatable truth is not technically a disagreeable thing any more than an impertinence, though, of course, the being told it is an unpleasant operation. It is necessary for us now and then to hear unpalatable and unwelcome truths; but a disagreeable thing is never a moral necessity, — it is spoken to relieve the speaker's mind, not to profit the hearer. The same utterance may be an impertinence, an unpalatable truth, or a disagreeable thing, according to time and circumstance. For example, in a fit of absence, we perpetrate some solecism in dress or behavior. It is an unwelcome truth to be told it, while there is yet opportunity for remedy, or partial remedy: it is an impertinence to be informed of it by a stranger who has no right to concern himself with our affairs: it is a disagreeable thing when — the occasion past — our friend enlightens us about it, simply as a piece of information. We all of us, no doubt, have friends, relations, and acquaintances who think it quite a sufficient reason for saying a thing, that it is true. Probably we have ourselves known the state of mind in which we find a certain fact or opinion a burden, a load to be got rid of; and, under the gross mistake that all truth must be spoken, that it is uncandid and dangerous not to deliver a testimony, — convinced that truth, like murder, will out, and that our friend, sooner or later, must learn the unacceptable fact, — we come to the conclusion that it is best for all parties to get the thing over by being ourself the executioner. We have most of us acted the *enfant terrible* at some time or other. But this crude simplicity of candor, where it is the result of the mere blind, intrusive assertion of truth, is a real weight; and the primary law of politeness, never to give unnecessary pain, as soon as it is apprehended, is welcomed as a deliverer. Children and the very young have not experience enough for any but the most limited sympathy, and can only partially compare the feelings of others with their own. Indeed, the idea of the comparison does not occur to them. But there are people who, in this respect, remain children all their days, and very awkward children too, — who burst with a fact as the fool with his secret, and, like the hair-dresser in Leech's caricature, are impelled to tell us that our hair is thin at the top, though nothing whatever is to come of the communication. These, as Sydney Smith says, turn friendship into a system of lawful and unpunishable impertinence, from, so far as we can see, no worse cause than incontinence of fact and opinion, — feeling it to be a sufficient and triumphant defence of every perpetration of the sort, that it is true. "Why did you tell Mr. So-and-so that his sermon was fifty minutes long?" "Because I had looked at my watch." "Why did you remind such a one that he is growing fat and old?" "Because he *is.*" "Why repeat that unfavorable criticism?" "I had just read it." "Why disparage this man's particular friends?" "I don't like them." "Why say to that young lady that her dress was unbecoming?" "I really thought so." It is, however, noticeable in persons of this obtrusive candor, that they have eyes for blemishes only. They are never impelled to tell pleasant truths, — from which, no doubt, we may infer a certain acerbity of temper, though these strictures may be spoken in seeming blunt, honest good-humor. Still, they talk in this way from natural obtuseness and inherent defect of sympathy. These are the people who always hit upon the wrong thing to say, and instinctively ferret out sore subjects. They are not the class we have in our thoughts. Indeed, they incapacitate themselves for serious mischief, as their acquaintance give them a wide berth, and take care not to expose their more cherished interests to their tender mercies. It requires some refinement of perception to say the more pungent and penetrating disagreeable things. We must care for the opinion or the regard of a person whose sayings of this sort can keenly annoy us. A man must have made friends before he can wound them. A real expert in this art is never rude, and can convey a disregard approaching to contempt for another's opinion, hit him in his most vulnerable points, and send him off generally depressed and uncomfortable, without saying a word that can be fairly taken hold of.

Of course the people most distinguished in this way are disappointed people. In the examples that occur to us, we perceive that life has not satisfied them, — they do not occupy the place in men's minds which they feel they deserve. But this is no explanation, for the tendency is just as likely to have caused the disappointment as the disappointment the tendency. People who start in life with high, though not wholly ungrounded notions of their own deserts, definite claims, and elaborate self-appreciation, are certain to be in constant collision with their friends, and with society. Their sense of their own rights and merits is perpetually infringed. Their friendship or service entails an obligation which is never duly recognized. The memory becomes loaded with supposed slights. Every part of the man is instinct with grievances, which inevitably exhale in disagreeable things. We hear them in covert insinuations. We read them in rigid smiles. They look out of cold, forbidding, eyes. They declare themselves in stiff, repelling courtesies. And the mischief does not end here. There is no habit more catching. Tempers amiable enough when let alone develop under a stimulus. It is not a wholly unpleasant excitement to find ourselves observing all the forms of friendly and kindly intercourse, yet giving as good as we get, or at any rate parrying with spirit. There is only one class of persons in the world, — the perfectly humble-minded, — who never say disagreeable things.

Nobody acknowledges himself to be an habitual offender in this line. No man will own himself careless of giving pain. When we do become conscious of having thoughtlessly wounded our neighbor's feelings or self-love, it may commonly be traced to the blinding sway of some conviction held in a one-sided, selfish spirit. All strong prepossessions destroy sympathy, and, like absence of mind, induce an exclusive attention to our own objects or wishes. To judge from their biographies, religious professors are exceedingly apt to err in this direction, — unless, perhaps, it be that they say disagreeable things more deliberately, and more on principle, than the laity. The young lady who answered her friend's announcement of her approaching marriage by the inquiry, if she had ever remembered that her future husband might die, thought she was preaching a sermon, but was simply saying a disagreeable thing. The occasion called for sympathy, and preaching was an obtrusion of self and its specialty, — an unconscious expedient for bringing down her friend from a high position of interest to a level something below her own. The habit of saying disagreeable things belongs impartially to both sexes, but the manner and the motive differ. Our example illustrates the feminine form. There is commonly a touch of jealousy to be traced in a woman's trying or irritating sayings, however remote and far-fetched. However abstract and general the remark may be, an insight into circumstances will probably furnish the clew, — will bring some personal and particular cause to light which has held sympathy in abeyance. Men can say disagreeable things without the suggestions of this prompter. They enjoy the pleasure of self-assertion, the gratification of putting a friend in possession of their exact impressions. There is a relish for taking down for its own sake a vein of hardness and cold-bloodedness, which belongs to some very respectable sort of people, impelling them to give a stone instead of bread, — to utter flinty "I told you so's," cold moralities, inopportune counsels, and harsh reminders, when the confiding spirit has laid bare its needs, or its penitence, and asked for sympathy. Often the mere knowledge of doing the thing well is motive enough.

It is an irresistible temptation to express one's self with point; and in fact, half of all the current good stories are of neatly turned disagreeable things, — not sneer or satire, but some cold, shivering half-truth, for which nobody is the better. Not that dull men are debarred from the indulgence, but they are clumsy, and slip at every turn into mere insolence or blunder. This is their secret of heavy banter, — which is nothing else than harping with stupid persistence on something unpleasant, with no other view than to make their object conscious of exposure, and for the moment smaller than themselves, — in contrast with the well-mannered jest which, under whatever disguise of depreciation, puts its subject in better humor with himself than he was before.

In a woman, this practice is not so much an exercise of the intellect as of the heart, speaking under some souring, embittering influence. Some are habitually ungracious from the working of vulgar rivalries, or mere grim acidity of nature. These are simply odious; but it is astonishing what things a woman sweet as summer will say, under certain conditions of the affections, to those most important to her, and for whom she cares most; and how seemingly unconscious she is of the tendency of her words, led on by jealous self-assertion and fancied ill-usage. There is a process of comparison peculiar to this mood, and which can express itself only by disagreeable things, —by a series of parallels and contrasts, in all of which she comes out the ascendant and superior. Perhaps new friends, in all their garish attractions, are contrasted with herself, the old, faithful, original friend, great in solid worth and refined feeling, or in unshaken fidelity. What chilling doubts, what cruel disparagement, what ingenuity of misapprehension attend this temper! What reflections on the constancy of her friends, what pity and contempt for their taste, what pathetic regrets, what resignation to the inevitable fate of a virtue, a spirit, a perception, which there is not steadiness, or wit, or heart to value at their true price! The worst of this strain, — the reason why this tone is so disagreeable, — is that it hits a blot. It is of the essence of disagreeable things that in some sense or degree they are true. This is why they irritate. For instance, our constancy is never so weak to our own consciousness as when our friends suspect it. We never see their social drawbacks clearer than when we are charged with being influenced by them. New friends are never in higher favor than when old friends upbraid us with them.

The main nursery for the science of disagreeable things is the domestic hearth. Here we do not note those distinctions of sex which strike us in society.

Men and women, husbands and wives, brothers and sisters, are apt to say very much the same class of disagreeable things to one another, unless good breeding or good temper interpose to prevent familiarity becoming contempt. It is wonderful what moral and refined writers assume to be family habits in this particular, from which we may suppose the practice to be more common than our state of civilization would lead us to hope. Certainly we all know, or have known, families where the strong tyrannize over the weak, and, in cold blood and in apparent good-nature, inflict perpetual minute wounds on the self-love of those about them. By this means, — like the Antiquary with his womankind, — a caustic temper keeps itself civil towards the outer world. A man can sustain his politeness to ladies in general by always calling his sister an old woman, or by constantly reminding her of events she would willingly forget. A woman can be gracious to her acquaintance and over-indulgent to her children by making her husband the vent of her ill-humors, — like Mrs. Glegg, installing herself the constituted check on his pleasures ; — while some people are agreeable to the whole world, except just those with whom they are connected by ties of blood, to whom they show a wholly different phase of character.

Sensitiveness to disagreeable things implies self-mistrust. Only absolutely self-reliant people are impervious to them. We are dependent on others more than we think for even our *own* good opinion. We think best of ourselves when others share our favorable impressions, and no strength of constancy can prevent our estimate of our friends suffering some faint fluctuations according to the view which others take of them. All people have an idea of their own position towards the world, — though "idea" is, perhaps, too definite a term, — at any rate, a dim assumption of a certain standing of which they are scarcely aware till it is infringed, and which it is the part of the sayer of disagreeable things to infringe. We are each the centre of our own world, and thus have a place in our own eyes which no one can give us. Something of this half-delusion is indispensable to carry us through our parts creditably, and the laws of politeness, on principle, support this degree of pretension. There is a tacit agreement in society that every individual in it fills his proper place, and that he and his belongings are what they go for, — that all our externals fulfil their professions. There is no hypocrisy in assuming this of every one we meet. It is simply not obtruding our private judgment where its expression would be an impertinence. The disagreeable thing jars on this nice adjustment. The speaker has the unjustifiable aim of lowering this fancied elevation, whether moral or social; and he dispels illusions, not, as he supposes, in the interest of truth on any social or moral view, but really for selfish ends. He obeys an unamiable impulse to prove that he is knowing where we are ignorant, wise where we are foolish, strong where we are weak,— that he sees into us and through us, and that it is, before all things, important that this should be declared and made evident.

On being Understood.

IF modesty would allow men to confess it, we do not doubt that it is a very common matter of surprise, — ingenuous surprise, and not a feeling really to be ashamed of, — why more people do not like us, care for us, show interest in us. It is very clear that most people have only a very limited number of admirers, and — not to speak of admirers — very few sympathizers, very few who find much pleasure in their society, or to whom they can feel of real consequence apart from the substantial services they can render, and beyond the domestic hearth, with which such speculations as these had best have nothing to do. Perhaps we are conscious of some play of thought, some kindness and largeness of heart, some capacities for sympathy, some tenderness and delicacy of feeling, some readiness of perception, some spark of fancy or humor only waiting to be kindled, some good-nature. How is it that others do not pay homage to such an array of good qualities? Some men think they are liked, — but they are not liked in the degree they suppose themselves to be. They are the objects of an amount of cold, patronizing good-will, but they have not the sort of thing we are meaning, and which so many of us honestly wonder we don't get. It does not signify much, — we do without it. We are not sure that violent appreciation would not be a bore, and entail a great deal of trouble. We would treat it as a scientific question rather than a want of the heart. It simply strikes us, one and all, when we come to think of it, as curious, how extremely few each man cares for, or gets to care for him, — how very few hit it together.

We have enumerated the good gifts of which every one is of course conscious; but we must in candor acknowledge that in mixed society we do not find them brought into play and exercised as we should beforehand expect them to be. Our wonder is, not so much that men do not greatly care for what they see in us, but how it happens that, as all these fine qualities are there, they do not contrive to find them out. As a fact, we are not appreciated. How comes that about? Why, we may ask with a pardonable warmth and indignation, do people *let* us be so dull and uninteresting in their presence, when we have it in us to be so different? There must certainly be a fault somewhere. If society were so ordered as to meet our idiosyncrasy, we should make a different appearance. It is becoming a pretty general discovery — and, therefore, we give it expression — that justice is not done. We are not brought out. We are suffered to smoulder. Our lamp is dim for want of air, — when, if we know ourselves, we have it in us to assist an illumination. Most concourses of men are dull. We have each reason to think it need not be so. We have called this a "discovery," because this cry of the soul is a feature of modern civilization. It seems clear that, in the days of our grandfathers, people used to meet and be entertained without the necessities we here hint at. A certain rude jollity and robustness of powers kept under the finer sensibilities. We do not deny that even now there are people who find society a field, who are courted, who shine, who, as the phrase is, make themselves agreeable. But this scarcely affects our argument; for is not the best talker that ever possessed the ear of a dinner-table careful to let us know that we see but the outside, that his inner self is never reached, that he all the while languishes for real sympathy, — that he has depths which a careless, laughing world takes no pains to search into?

We believe that, if Dr. Johnson lived in our time

he would consider himself not understood, — an idea, as far as we can see, that never once entered his head, after the world took him up; and we have no doubt that this conviction would have hampered his flow, and, so to say, shut him up in many a company where he made the grandest figure. And this probably explains why there are no Dr. Johnsons now, and no anybodies of that sort. People were not in those days so dependent on somebody to draw them out. In another point, there is a difference. If our vanity is not less exacting than theirs, it is more fastidious. A man in these days is jealous of being listened to and cared for merely as a lion, merely as an author. The idea is that there is something beyond what shows itself in work achieved, — something more intensely the man's self than what comes out of him. When Cumberland intimated that he wanted to be treated, not as a writer of plays, but as a gentleman, the world of his day did not know what he was at, and thought he gave himself airs; but every successful author would say so now, and every one would take the feeling for granted. Not that our fathers were wholly without the notion of getting at a man, or unconscious that some had this gift more than others, but they still did not touch our modern strain. Thus it was said of Sir Walter Scott, that he could not travel with a man in a coach without learning something from him. No doubt he could have learnt something from us, but would he have understood us? There is the question. It is not what we know, but what we *are,* that is at the root of this sensitive aspiration. A desire to reveal our very inside of all — with, at the same time, a bashful recoil from the operation — characterizes the modern mind, which, in despair of individual sympathy, often throws itself upon the public as the only true confidant; so that the more reserve prevails in society, each member of which we know just a little, the more we seem ready to reveal our secrets to our readers and hearers, — if they are only in crowds enough, — of whom individually we know nothing.

Some good souls, approaching this question, have said that there is something in everybody that will repay the trouble of investigation if it could only be got at. Our experience, we own, does not reach so far. The Germans — who, as Charles Lamb says, are profounder than we — have theorized prettily on the mystery of dulness, which they cannot believe in as a process of nature. Thus, Tieck describes or conceives of a conversational alchemist whose "richly intellectual discourse made everybody who talked with him clear-headed and clever"; and he goes on to assert, that there is some fruitful soil in every mind which should bring forth peculiar products, and from which the originality of the individual should proceed. In most cases, he grants, this has been checked by neglect or conventional culture. He complains, beside, that most conversations have simply for their object that each should hear himself speak, without any desire that the other should express either his outer or his inner mind. "But where a master in the science of men chances to touch these wasted instruments, he knows how to draw wondrous tones even from the most spoiled." This word "wondrous" explains the want of the age. It is the mystic "inner self" that must somehow be drawn forth. Not that we profess to go all lengths with the German in the universality of these precious qualities. It is a theory which certainly does not commend itself to general acceptance; for we see that the desire to reveal the inner self tends rather to a monopoly, — that is, the craving to be understood leads inevitably in practice to the formation of cliques. The word is not in good favor; but the thing, however, demoralizing, we believe to be exceedingly agreeable. When a few people get together with this view, there springs out of the intercourse a satisfaction, not to say elation, not to be attained in any other way. It is impossible to get the appreciation of the whole world; but it is easy to think a very few people all the world to us. Where a coterie is established under a tacit agreement that each member shall be understood, there springs a sense of importance and consequent indulgence of every man's humor, a worship of characteristics, a reckless self-reliance, a fearlessness and *abandon* of expression, a disregard and even forgetfulness of every way of viewing things out of the charmed circle, which is more like liberty, community, and fraternity, than we can expect to find elsewhere. We are sure of sanction; we are radiant with genial *esprit de corps;* there is a community of thought and achievement. We may be foolish, but what of that? we feel clever; and, moreover, we *are* cleverer, — our thoughts more vivacious, our intelligence more ready, in the particular groove that we have assigned to it. The historical French coteries may be ridiculous to look back upon, — may have strayed into unbounded extravagances; but how clever they were, and how they did enjoy themselves, and look down upon the rest of the world! And our own literary annals show similar combinations, on the same principle of making it everybody's interest to extol, draw out, set off the other. Nothing can be more cold and chill than the outer world to one of these cockered, indulged, drawn-out spirits, beyond the prestige of its own circle; but the tendency of the world is to defer to people who set store by themselves, and a coterie of sufficient spirit and pretension secures for itself real serviceable reputation, though the excluded may affect satire, and indulge in word-disparagement.

But the real triumphs of a coterie, and what comes of it when people *do* understand one another to the backbone, must be looked for in another hemisphere. In this our American cousins go ahead, as in everything else, unimpeded by the phlegm of the old world, and armed in a panoply of self-confidence, really glorious in its unconscious daring. The circle we have now more especially in view has Mr. Emerson for its historian, and had Margaret Fuller for its priestess. In the depth and niceness of penetration which intimate knowledge of each other induced, we must not wonder that this school uses language as yet obscure to the uninitiated. Thus the lady had one fault, — that she was "too intellectual, and too conscious of intellectual relation, so that she was not sufficiently self-centred in her own personality, and hence something of duality"; but whether we can understand her or not, it is clear she had the gift we desire in our friends. "No one ever came so near"; "her mood applied itself to the mood of her companion, point by point, in the most limber, sinuous, vital way"; "she applied herself to the mood of her companion as the sponge applies itself to water," and the results are just what each one craves for himself:—"You fancy you know D.," she writes. "It is too absurd; you have never seen him. When I found him here sitting like a statue I was alarmed; thought him ill. You sit with courteous, *un*confiding smile, and suppose him to be a mere man of talent. He is so with you. But the moment I was alone with him he was another creature. His manner, so glassy and elaborate before, was full of soul, and the tones of his voice entirely different."

"And I have no doubt," said Mr. Emerson, "that she saw expressions, heard tones, and received thoughts from her companions, which no one ever heard from the same *parties*." (So he writes it.) But if she was this to the uninitiated, to lovers and artists, gray statesmen, old aunts, coach travellers,—if they one and all found themselves turning over their most secret treasures for her inspection,—how was it with the congenial circle of kindred spirits? We can only assure our readers that the subjects of discussion in that circle, and the way of treating them, as reported to us, are so great, so stupendous, so deep, so vast, so comprehensive of all that nature has to show, so exhaustive of all that philosophers have thought and poets have dreamt, that one page of the inspired "Margaret" and her coterie seems to embrace the universe. And, what is much to our point,—as proving the stimulating effects of forming one of a charmed and perfectly understood circle, — whatever the subject, whether the question is, What is life? or, What particular view had people in worshipping Bacchus or Apollo? whether the discourse turns on the soul of beauty, or searches into the very secrets of the fine arts, or dives into the abyss of motives, all the members of the little society were equal to the occasion, and could say something positively clever. Such are the magical effects of an exact pervading sympathy. "All satisfied her," and all with whom she conversed surprised her by their power; though, as her historian candidly confesses, "we were all obliged to recall Margaret's testimony when we found we were sad blockheads to other people."

But in showing that American transcendentalists are clever, we seem to have wandered worlds away from our starting-point, which asked why *we* are dull. We have not, after all, the least wish to be demigods like Mr. Emerson; but why have we nothing to say to our acquaintance of twenty years' standing? We talk of subjects that interest us, and on which we could say something. Why do we not say it? Why would not our friend care to hear it if we did? And we, in our turn, why are we so dead to merits in him that other people vouch for? Each is sensible of a glow, a fervor, a sparkle, which keeps himself warm,

— why is it so feeble a glimmer to the other? The intercourse of mind is a mystery; what are the barriers so invisible, yet so invincible, which make association so often a mere trial and delusion! We meet only at points, — we touch only with our claws, — we are justified in denouncing each the other as a heavy fellow, for so in truth we are.

We suppose it is a continuance of that great necessary evil, that unsocial decree promulged at the Tower of Babel. Possibly, the pressure of this primeval ordinance takes from us any strong constraining desire to please, except under circumstances tempting to our vanity, and makes us realize the trouble of being agreeable, — which is, indeed, to not a few the hardest thing they are ever put to. The world must be peopled, and if every man had liked his neighbor, enjoyed his company, and found something to say to him, people would have stuck together like bees in a swarm, and three parts of the earth to this day would have been desert.

Study of Character.

WE hear a great deal about knowledge of character, and it is, no doubt, a fine thing to suppose ourselves possessed of an insight into the motives and interior mechanism of all our acquaintance; but we have not that entire faith in it as a genuine attainment, — as a practical, substantial benefit, as a protection from mistake, as a guide through life, with which its pretensions ought to inspire us. The characters men draw in books hang together in a wonderful harmony of parts. If we had to deal with them we should know what we were about. They are amazingly consistent, and we exclaim, How natural! what a wonderful knowledge of human nature has Scott, or Richardson, or Dickens, or Charlotte Brontë! But the difficulty in real life is that people are not natural, — that they are inconsistent, — that their deviations from their proper selves would disgrace a novel and spoil any author's reputation.

Take some men and compare them one year with another, one day with another, and there is absolutely scarce a trace of the former man. Hamlet puzzles the commentators because he is not always reconcilable with himself; but, surely, all of us can point out some one or more compared with whom Hamlet is plain sailing. We suspect that great artists, attempting to draw from life, feel this, — are embarrassed with the incongruities and perversities of humanity, and have to convey an idea as they can, by antithesis and by uniting opposites. Even Shakespeare has to describe Wolsey by this method. We may always detect a real character amongst shadows in a novel by his want of harmony. The more true he is to the writer's observation, the less natural he is, — that is, if it be nature for your actions to follow in a sort of necessary sequence from your qualities. So Pope felt embarrassed with his mighty subject, and hopeless of reducing the study to a science: —

> "See the same man in vigor, or the gout,
> Alone, in company, in place or out;
> Early at business, and at hazard late,
> Mad at a fox-hunt, wise at a debate;
> Drunk at a borough, civil at a ball,
> Friendly at Hackney, faithless at Whitehall."

It is impossible to draw such characters. They are either a satire, like Pope's Wharton and Dryden's

Villiers, or they are slurred over, all blemishes and puzzles lost under a glaze of encomium. Charles Lamb has a pretty attempt at a portrait of an uncle in "My Relations," wherein "he limps," after Sterne, "in my poor antithetical manner, as the fates have given me grace and talents"; but the result is, that we feel the man would be intolerable to us, though the writer "would not have him one jot or tittle other than he is." Thus he has failed to convey his idea, as every one must who attempts to draw a character by the process of pairing contradictory qualities.

From Bacon's Essays we might infer that men studied character in his day with a very deliberate intention of getting some substantial good by it. He has a dozen excellent recipes for turning a man round your thumb. "If you would work any man, you must either know his nature or his fashions, and so lead him; or his ends, and so persuade him; or his weakness and disadvantages, and so awe him," and so on; but it has been found that arts reduced to rule do not go much way in informing men what is within the smooth exterior of their friends and neighbors. No doubt experience teaches men, under favorable circumstances, to get the knack of all this, though diplomatists have left off imparting their discoveries; but the study of character does not progress as a written science. Not inquiries into the nature of man, physiognomy, phrenology, theories of temperaments, nor the rest of it, advance us one step beyond the old instinct which belongs to some people, and not to others, which fails the oftenest in all difficult crises, and which no one can impart to his fellow. However, every one assumes himself to have a share of this instinct. Few of us would like to be supposed wholly in the dark as to the inner workings of the minds with which we have to do, though the knowledge we assume implies some sense of partial superiority, the presumption of some vantage-ground lifting us above the object of our survey. We read, we interpret, we combine, we reconcile, we penetrate, and, consciously or unconsciously, we are perpetually occupied with the distinct features and peculiarities of that portion of the human family that comes under our observation. Perhaps when most earnestly at work we are least aware of what we are doing. The more intimate and habitual our scrutiny, and the more interest or affection stimulate and quicken our perception, the less we realize our occupation. Domestic affection, indeed, has lost some of its delicacy when members of a family get up one another's character from the point of view of a deliberate survey. Still, we do come to such an acquaintance with our subject that we may be said to know him in that phase of life under which we contemplate him ; but here we stop. Knowledge of character, to be real, — to show true, thorough insight, — ought to be able to prophesy; it ought to embrace such a view of principles of action, inborn and acquired qualities, natural bias and subjection to influence, as to be able to foresee how circumstances will tell on any mind or temper with which we profess to be acquainted. But who can do this? Who can separate native character from the bands of habit and the ties of society? Which of us knows himself so well as to guess what he would be, and do, and think, when put out of his present way of life? — much less what others would do; whatever may be said of self-deception, it is certain that every man knows secrets about himself which no one else has surmised, and which are indispensable to the foresight of which we speak.

Recognized knowledge of character is an attainment, and, if real, is founded on instinct quickened by observation, experience, or interest. The very word character is not understood without education. Amongst people who have no discernment, or who do not use it in the selection of their choicer phrases, character is, like "individual," or "party," a synonyme for man or woman. Thus we have heard a fat old man defined as a "stout character." With a vast many people the word has a simply technical, marketable value, and, standing alone, implies the assemblage of moral and physical qualities which make a good cook or butler. With the police it has a wholly opposite signification, and calling a man a character is giving him a bad name, and next to hanging. All who come under their cognizance as dangerous members of the community are *characters.* The persons who, if they know no harm of them, are *parties*, are *characters* if they do. Thus they talk of fighting characters, disorderly characters, characters on a race-course, lodging-houses full of characters, and so on. Nor is this use of the term, in its spirit, wholly without precedent in the classes above them. There are many people who regard anything erratic, any quality in a man which marks him different from his fellows, anything characteristic, as something questionable and to be shunned. Their idea of praise is to say that a man has no peculiarities. When they like a person, their mode of expressing their liking is to divest him of every distinctive feature. If a man, he is as good a fellow as ever walked; if a woman, as nice a little woman as ever lived; if a girl, she falls under the universal encomiums of "good-natured," "unaffected," "with no nonsense about her"; while their ideal in every case is absolute uniformity to the common standard, and "always the same" comprises all they have to bestow of commendation. In fact, to a good many people, any new or unexpected exhibition of character is painful from their utter inability to make it out. The language of tempers, minds, and qualities, is one for which they have neither grammar nor dictionary. They don't know what may be going to happen to them when they see them at work, to what amount of humiliation and discomfort such strange novelties may not subject them. In their case this dread may be a safeguard; there is a great risk in having to do with people who can't be classed, — with strong qualities which they choose to direct in their own independent fashion. And this no doubt accounts for what we have often observed, — that a practised insight into the minds and tempers of others does not preserve men from great mistakes, from taking up people whom they have to lay down again, from sudden friendships, and as sudden coolings. Indeed, the more conspicuous mistakes of this sort we have in our eye are of people who justly pique themselves on their penetration. Complex characters, so alarming to the incurious, are the delight of the professed student of his species. We all, as we have said, know people who will not come under any definition, either for good or evil, — who can't be described in few words, who are made up of opposites, to whom we can find no clew, who are forever perplexing us, always running counter to our previous opinion, baffling our foresight and sagacity. These never get fair treatment from people who like to form a judgment at a glance, who believe in transparent characters, and talk of windows in men's breasts. But the student does not object to sinuosities and obscurities, is not offended by a touch of the Jesuit, hails every difficulty as a stimulus to his ingenuity, and naturally likes to set his individual discernment against the judgment of a blundering and illiberal world.

Of course, there are no absolutely transparent characters. They are as pure an invention as that other fiction of infallible readers of character. There is something in every man of which we have no consciousness, hid from himself and hid from us, and which nothing but the event will lay bare. Nobody, whatever his penetration, can be sure what his best friend, or the man he knows best, will do under untried or startling circumstances. Some influence counter to all he has had the opportunity to observe asserts itself in the crisis and contradicts every foregone conclusion. Experience, of course, is better able to cope with new situations, but only in showing that, when we are beyond our actual knowledge, it is safer to rely on the impulses common to all men than on the consistent working of individual character. Thus it is found neither wise nor safe to assume anybody, whatever the extent of our observation, to be quite above the motives of action incident to his new sphere; and while the most agreeable manner goes on the assumption of our being what we ought to be, the most judicious calculations are made on the principle that our friend will be influenced by what influences the mass of mankind. Again, no training, nor instinct even, can enable a man to comprehend any character in those points which are beyond his reach. There are a dozen sorts of knowledge, all accurate in their way, each taking up a character from a different point of view. Men's weakness and faults, says Bacon again, "are best known to their enemies; their virtues and abilities to their friends; their customs and times from their servants; their conceits and opinions from their familiar friends with whom they discourse most."

> "How many pictures of one 'mind' we view,
> All how unlike each other, all how true!"

A narrow yet penetrating intellect sees a certain way into a higher intelligence, but beyond that is in the dark, and that which is beyond may involve the deepest and most distinctive parts of the man. Satire constantly works in this way, — not only the keen, pointed satire we find in books, but the frivolous, shallow satire of private life, — true as far as it goes, but not attaining to the real inner man at all.

If, then, study of character can go so little way, — if it so poorly fulfils its pretensions, — what is its use and purpose? No doubt things may be very useful in their degree without doing all they profess to do. We should jostle one another frightfully without some perceptions of character. Imperfect as it is, it is of enormous social value, but, then, rather as tact than insight. Women are, we suspect, the most indefatigable students of character, though not the most systematic. They are this without knowing it. Thus we see them looking up to the men about them — husband, lover, or brother — as heroes, and all the while acting on a minute acquaintance with a tribe of repulsive or unamiable faults. They will act on the knowledge that a man is mean, envious, jealous, malignant, ill-tempered, and never seem to know a word of it, — will screen him, humor him, use all their tact to keep his failings out of sight, and actually at the same time *think* him magnanimous. But also they are conscious students. It is wonderful with what patient investigation a keen-sighted woman will set herself to reach the motives and depths of some character that interests her. The subject may not, perhaps, to the masculine apprehension, be especially worthy of so much pains, but in some incomprehensible way he may hit her turn for hero-worship. We submit that the distinction does not always go by merit, nor yet by success. Let it only be a "fine natural character" in which the war of temperaments has fair play, — let only strength and weakness, gentleness and obstinacy, energy and indolence, power and helplessness, show themselves by turns unchecked by too stringent a self-discipline, — and she sits as at a tournament. Of course a certain belief in some intrinsic greatness or other sustains her curiosity. She assumes that the puzzle is worth finding out, — which the secret of all this reserve, or sadness, or impetuosity, or harshness does not always prove to be. But it is a labor that brings its own reward in her case as in all others. The study of character may not have such substantial benefits as some suppose, — it may not place its votary beyond the risk of being deceived. The student may, and often is, taken in by a knave, and mistaken in a friend, and out in his reckonings, but he is always amused. To him, and him alone, all the world 's a stage and life a drama. He is forever at the play. He is sustained, too, by a constant sense of superiority, — he is always in the lofty attitude of a judge. What irritates others is to him only food for speculation. Indeed, we do not see what right a man has ever to be taken by surprise or to get angry with those actions in others which are in accordance with his preconceived notions of character, even though they may be performed upon himself; while, if they are contrary to his justly grounded expectations, here is a mystery to solve, a new phase to study, an intricacy to unravel, which should keep his intellect clear and temper cool, though the unenlightened are in a passion. And, last, in the intercourse of every day he is at an enormous advantage. He need make no blunders and tread on no one's toes. While we plod on in the dark, he has an inner light always showing him the way. Nor need he ever find society dull. Everybody has a character of some sort, and a thousand to one but there are points in it which will well repay the pains of investigation. It is the unobservant alone that never find anything interesting, curious, or wonderful in their path.

PREJUDICES.

IT is part of human nature to hedge about everything it loves with restrictions. We cannot like a thing without isolating it from what we do not like. We are driven at once to comparisons, which, by enhancing what we care for, lower something else, so that what was before simply indifferent becomes objectionable. If we have likes, we must have dislikes; if we have strong light, we must have shadow. These dislikes, these shadows, these exclusions, are our prejudices. We do not feel the full worth of what we value till there is something which by contrast we despise. Warm sympathies are not found without a capacity for strong antipathies. There are people, no doubt, who begin from the other end,—who, through satiety or disgust at what they know, prefer the unknown, whose prejudices are not the opposites of their likings, but hatreds and antipathies at first hand. Cynicism and misanthropy, however, are not acknowledged sources of prejudice. Their workings go by another name; they are malignant and aggressive, and tend to actual mischief. Even at best, prejudices cannot be so defined in words as to look well. They are cramping, narrowing things, incompatible with perfect justice and charity. The man who loves his country till he despises all other countries is very apt to love his county till he despises all other counties, and his parish, or his clan, or his family, to the exclusion of every other parish, clan, and family, till the amount of love in his heart will bear no proportion to the contempt generated and kept in action by this perpetual process of comparison. Even in moderation, and as the most respectable people hold their prejudices, we all trust in a higher transcendent state to be without them; and nobody of decent feeling but looks forward to more than tolerating in another world the sight, and possibly the companionship, of persons against whom he entertains the strongest present prejudice. But, nevertheless, we do not see how prejudices are altogether to be dispensed with in this sublunary sphere. They are an inseparable element of human weakness, which would be still weaker and more helpless without them. Who is so open to every temptation as the man who boasts himself to have outgrown every prejudice incident to his birth and training? The very notion of being thus divested, even if it were possible, which it is not, is that of living in a glass house, — a bare, shivering, comfortless cosmopolitanism. It is well to be modest about our prejudices, as vaguely conscious that they will not stand reason's cold pervading daylight; but a studious and comprehensive renunciation is like giving up ownership and personal appropriation in our surroundings. It is quarrelling with the very ground we stand on, because it does not put us at an elevation commanding an unbroken horizon. We would rather be the victim of every insular prejudice than have no British preferences. It would argue higher powers of appreciation, and a clearer perception; for the merits of the best things do not lie on the surface, — experience alone acquaints us with them. Therefore, as far as we know, the country we are happy in *is* immeasurably superior to others which we know less, or are wholly ignorant of. It is this full appreciation of what is known which makes critics of all ages so subject to prejudice, — which is the zeal of partial knowledge, — and the best of them only infallible in the manner with which they are familiar. Intense pleasure in, and comprehension of, certain forms of grace, beauty, and perfection have a tendency to restrict the mind to those particular forms and methods which first opened the mind to such influences. It is easy for a man to be fair and candid between rival poets or painters or styles, if he has not eye or ear or thought fully to appreciate any. We may wonder at Addison now for his almost insolent expression of preference of Grecian over Gothic architecture; but we do not doubt his imagination "was filled with something great and amazing" in entering the Pantheon, — a thrill which the building is worthy to inspire, but which it needs a finer and more cultivated taste to experience than is possessed by many a reader who despises the prejudices of cold classicism. Mr. Ruskin's prejudices would make even tolerance intolerant; but unquestionably his admiration of Turner, though in a good degree merited by its object, is beyond the capacity of an ordinary observer, who thinks himself more reasonable while he is certainly less discerning. Jeffrey's persecution of Wordsworth was partly due to his ear and heart being preoccupied by the sweetness of other melodies that had but a slight hold on duller senses, which for this reason were more open to new, but probably still feeble, impressions. To us the point of regret is, not when these prejudices are strong, and so vigorously maintained that they carry persuasion with them, but when, as we sometimes see, the critic develops unexpected caprice, turns upon himself, is spiteful on his old idol, and confounds his followers by an utter retractation. This is a spectacle to weaken our faith in man. What has been forcibly expressed has not, it seems, been strongly felt. In fact, a man never makes a poorer figure than in thus unscrupulously discarding as prejudices what he had impressed upon others as convictions. While he parades his emancipation with the airy elation which belongs to this attitude of mind, we think him shallow and trivial. He has, after all, seen no deeper into things than we have; his confidence has been but a knack, a trick of the tongue. It does not happen to the stronger class of minds — minds privileged to influence others — thus to turn round upon their own congenial prejudices. There is too much truth in them as they see them.

It is a great misfortune, and perhaps one of the greatest trials that can befall a keen original mind, to be born in an atmosphere of mean or narrow prejudices, — for the one reason amongst others, that there is peril in the act of casting them off. Our notions, and even our beliefs, are bound up in one bundle. Untie the string, and there is a general scattering. A prejudice hastily got rid of imparts to all who are not gifted with an exceptional discretion, a wild sense of freedom extremely apt to degenerate into license. It is this that has made the more prudent minds of every age submissive to its prejudices. Rebellion is such an extreme measure, puts the mind in such a questionable frame, that it must be reserved for essentials. There are not many people who would be the better for the sudden loss of every unreasonable habit of thought. We see some examples in our day of this form of enlightenment, and they are not encouraging. When a man, and more especially when a woman, awakes to the conviction that he or she has been the dupe, through youth and dawning thought, of a string of absurd restrictions, superstitious observances, and useless sacrifices, — has been held the slave of local or family traditions, which owe all their credit to custom and all their weight to the fact that they have never yet been disputed, — the reaction of independence is a dangerous transition. It has happened to able and witty exponents of prejudice to show in their own persons that it might have been well for them to have retained every stupid check and heavy fetter of their youth. Illumination on the tyranny of custom leaves some minds defenceless against invasion from every opposing quarter, till each tie seems a prejudice and a trammel to be discarded. The people, they are ready to argue, who held mistaken ideas as to what constitutes prudence in affairs, and on the right modes of spending time, and on rules of social conduct, and who clung to their delusions as the soberest and most respectable of truths, may also have been mistaken in their rigid morality and implicit religious faith. The floodgates of doubt are opened, — a spirit of scepticism opposes itself to the old dogmatism. The mind which feels that it has been taken in allows itself to extend the bounds of supposed deception, and sets up a standard of virtue, which, in more points than we care to specify, is a departure from the old ideal.

The habit thus formed of subjecting every time-honored belief and principle of action to the ever-sitting tribunal of a man's own reason, under the pressure of present influences and temptations, is a worse habit, for all minds but the highest, than unreasoning submission to custom. There are very few indeed who can carry things in absolute suspense till the judgment has given its award. For, after all, most prejudices have some discipline and restraint in them; they cannot be indulged but at some expense and sacrifice. We hear of men being the slaves of their prejudices, which implies that they forego for their sake what would otherwise be agreeable. Thus, many old people, under this stern domination, refuse themselves all the comfort which relaxation of posture would afford them. They will persist in sitting bolt upright, not because it is not pleasant to lean back in an easy chair, or repose on a sofa, but because they have a prejudice which they like better than bodily ease. Who can over-estimate the sacrifice to an idea, however mistily apprehended, of that female politician who, we are told, parted with the best cook in England because the woman had said something to her fellow-servants that seemed to favor the suspension of the Habeas Corpus Act! When the Irish were starving in hopeless famine, they clung to their prejudice against sucking-pig. They and the pigs might die of hunger, but they would not lower themselves so far in their own eyes as to prolong life by such means, however tempting to grosser instincts. In this way prejudices are a constant source of content, rendering men contemptuous to all forms of novelty, and more than reconciling them to things as they are, even where change holds out the premium of undoubted physical advantages. But for this, how would certain portions of the earth's surface remain inhabited? how would many a life of restraint be cheerfully endured? For this reason, the inconvenient prejudices of subordinates are often favored as signs of honesty and sincerity, and proofs of their being guided by higher principles than those of cold self-interest.

It is not easy to distinguish refinement — a fastidious rejection of a hundred things for which severe reason can give no account — from prejudice. Especially feminine delicacy, and much of the niceness and particularity which makes women graceful and charming, seems to have a touch of prejudice in it. Thus travelling, seeing the world, roughing it, as it is called, are commended by the bolder and more independent spirits of the sex, for the special reason that they rub off prejudice, and correct the mere blind caution of ignorance. Results, however, tend to prove that what they call prejudices, and what in discussion look like them, are but veiled truths, subtly adapted to the nature that holds them, but too fine, complicated, and delicate for argument and definition. It is a suspicion of this that makes men consider the least accountable prejudices as the dearest part of themselves, as conveying a sense of intuitive knowledge. And things are so constituted in this world, everything is so permeated with imperfections, that, when driven hard, a reason and defence, — an excuse, at least, — for the most flagrant, can generally be found. An ingenious person never wants food and sanction for the maintenance of his prejudices. "Does not this," asks Dr. Johnson, "confirm old Meynell's observation, — 'For anything I see, foreigners are fools'?" And an old lady, lamenting the disappearance of wigs, found very presentable arguments in proof of her assertion, that, "Now all men wear their own hair, you never know one man from another." As a very needful clog upon change, indeed, we always welcome the prejudices of the old. What would become of us if there were not some to maintain that old things are better than new? But there are some who, in this respect, are always old, — who are born antiquarians. It is wonderful, where the mind is of this order, how soon a compact phalanx of prejudices, an invincible jealousy of innovation, will be formed; and how what has once, in earliest years, recommended itself as fitting, will establish itself as the ideal, never to be departed from. Where this habit belongs to a sensitive temperament, quick to apprehend and strong to retain, it forms an interesting and influential character; but it is essential that the prejudices should be the opposites of strong, just, and spontaneous likings. The most mischievous prejudices, carried on from generation to generation, are not of this order. They are those of interest rather than feeling, and are indulged for the holder's own ease and profit. Such are the prejudices of class against class, of the landed interest against trade, of the privileged against those who threaten to destroy their monopoly. These are, many of them, selfish at the core, though what is selfish, as one man holds it, may be but a distorted manifestation of a true principle as maintained by another. It may be loyalty and devotion rendered ugly and grotesque by faults of training and narrow intellect. When Lady Margaret Bellenden would have plunged her Whig prisoner into her "pit or principal dungeon, which, as being only two storeys under ground, could not be unwholesome," it argued no unnatural cruelty. Her mind was warped from its nature by strong party prejudice, which would not suffer her to realize that Covenanters were men. And popular prejudices have sanctioned the grossest tyrannies and the most revolting cruelty from the same blinding cause, though unquestionably the habit of such prejudice might, if left to itself without any counteracting influences, result in another Kingdom of Dahomey, which has lately been indulged with a sacrifice of two thousand human beings simply in deference to a national prejudice, and to keep up the good old customs of the country.

Perhaps men's most virulent prejudices have a close affinity with what they most care for, from which they are separated by an invisible line. Thus, religious parties that hold *almost* every belief in common, hate one another most fervently; and even where a man neither knows his own opinions nor those of his theological opponent, it is very possible for a strong prejudice to exist, founded on a mere supposition of minute difference. Indeed, a good many people's religion is mainly seen in the number and violence of ignorant antipathies. Except that persons cannot be detached from things, one might say that people may have what prejudices they please but personal ones, so long as they do not interfere with the rights of others, and that private people may extend the privilege to persons out of their sphere. How, for example, can we grudge the rustic politician some unfounded ideas about Mr. Gladstone or Lord Russell? But prejudices that doggedly maintain themselves under real intercourse are dangerous, evil things. To be consciously the object of a prejudice is of all things the most discouraging, and the most certain to bring about its own justification: for who can act according to his best nature under hostile observation? We have assumed that all people, as being mortal, have some prejudices, nor do we wish our friends to occupy themselves in a perpetual eradication of every feeling, liking, or opinion for which they cannot give a reason that shall convince all the world; but it is mean to be the slaves and victims of prejudice. A generous nature always shows that it is master over its prejudices, — that it can, upon occasion, act in direct opposition to the most cherished of them, and sweep them aside at will. Thus, opposing heads of parties often astonish their followers by an almost ostentatious magnanimity, when brought face to face and within sight of each other's great qualities; and, in fact, there is an effusion and sudden sense of enlargement, evidently very agreeable while it lasts, in these transient amnesties, — sometimes even betraying the principals, drawn towards each other by a sense of kindred gifts, into an expression of contempt for the restricted sympathies which own their sway. And the snub, though ungracious, has its uses, as impressing a needful lesson of liberality, free from that danger to the partisan's humility which we have seen to be a frequent attendant on the flash of enlightenment and the too hasty divestment of prejudice.

Shirking.

THERE is a form of evasion which can only be succinctly expressed by the word we have ventured to place at the head of this paper. Human weakness naturally has recourse to slang, as being tender and indulgent in its satire, with no derivations telling awkward tales and bringing ugly charges; but if there is a word to be found in any dictionary that means the same thing as that we conceive to be forced upon us, our apology must be that we do not know it. Procrastination, that thief of time, is no doubt head and chief of shirkers in act and performance, and makes more shirkers than any other influence. But at its worst it only shows the passive form, and says To-morrow, and to-morrow, and to-morrow. It does not even whisper to itself "Never," — its one change from the old cry is the hypocritical "Too late." The procrastinator, then, does shirk, but the shirker proper intends to shirk, and takes a resolve.

Both states of mind recognize a duty, and own an obligation, which neither performs; but the one always feebly means to do it, while the other as feebly concludes to do it not. Both faintly outrage conscience, both infuse a sneaking sense of qualm and failure; and if, morally, procrastination has the best of it from the presence of some ineffectual good intention, shirking, on the other hand, by owning the dignity of a resolution, however indefensible, in some sort strikes a balance. We give this as a point of difference; it may not, however, *be* the difference it seems. Neither we nor the man himself can ever be sure he meant to do a thing till he does it. It may only be that the procrastinator is always expecting fate to interpose some obstacle to the disagreeable duty, while the shirker learns to regard himself as his own fate.

We have taken procrastination as one word that might be substituted for that of our choice, because so many who shirk attribute their failure to this cause, and because many historical examples were procrastinators. Hamlet, in our eyes, was not mad, but he shirked a task imposed upon him; and his mind, being of heroic proportions, suffered the pangs of indecision in a heroic degree. Coleridge and DeQuincey were procrastinators, and also shirkers of every duty and responsibility that either nature or their own act involved them in. But, in fact, there are a hundred other motives to shirk what is unpleasant. We are by no means all of us procrastinators, but we *are* all of us shirkers, as being men. No temperament can save us. Only the best men, and those most under discipline, do not shirk in great things. There are people, indeed, who, seen at their best, and not too near, might seem to escape this pusillanimity of our nature, — who wish to do *all* things like men, not only their show and conspicuous actions, — who might appear to live by the precept, —

> " When thou dost purpose aught within thy power,
> Be sure to do it, though it be but small " ;

but we cannot live with them without finding, or even without having forced on us, a weak place somewhere, just to show that they are of the same flesh and blood.

It does not do to say of a merely selfish person, that he shirks his duties: a man must have feeling and conscience to realize them first. Nor is it, perhaps, correct to speak of any one shirking great acknowledged duties ; for, if they are shirked, it is as not owning their true importance. Harsh, rough, and brutal natures ignore and disown their obligations, — they do not shirk them ; this is the part of metaphysicians, who can explain everything away, and of amiable persons, men of sensibility and refinement, whose resolution is not equal to their perception of right. Imagination, indeed, is a great assistant to this posture of mind. A ready power of conjuring up possible contingencies makes some people shirk very obvious, and what, to most men, seem easy duties. The possibility of something disagreeable happening is a much greater terror to many, perhaps to most, than the actual calamity would be; and if, instead of doing a thing that has to be done, a man once sets himself to consider all the possible difficulties and embarrassments that may attend the performance, he will never do it at all. All the people we know as shirkers are persons who have a very keen appreciation of the disagreeable, and find many things intolerable which active working minds disregard. They are even disinterestedly alive to the dangers and horrors of certain lines of action. They cannot understand going ahead against a nameless fear, and would shirk for others as they do for themselves.

The most successful men, we are disposed to think, are those of an exactly opposite temperament, who have force and clear-sightedness to see the advantage of shirking nothing, — the clear sight, we mean, of common sense. Thus, men called *par excellence* "worldly," often shame those who call them so by their unflinching conduct under natural temptations to shirk, — under annoyances, wounds to pride and consequence, or irksome exactions on their time and patience, — under a hundred provocations that false shame would yield to. By this means they learn the real bearing of things, and shake off the disabling suggestions of an exaggerating morbid fancy. It is much better policy, for instance, to own everything about yourself, even in a worldly point of view, than to have any shuffling disguises; but people who shirk never see this, and no doubt it needs singular and unusual strength and decision to act on this rule, to see the eventual economy of wear and tear in never shirking. These are the men, however, who take the tide at the full, — the tide that leads to fortune. The charge of nepotism so constantly brought against the self-made men of history is a proof of this. A Pope, instead of ignoring his humbler relations, owns them. Napoleon, instead of hushing down his brothers and sisters, made them kings and queens. The strength that leads to rule and empire has this characteristic, — it is a nobleness of nature, compatible with the utmost degree of unscrupulousness. In fact, it often is simply courage and an enlarged self-interest, — no moral virtue at all. We cannot say that the honesty with which the actual state of things is accepted, as a basis to be built upon, marks the difference between high and low, good and bad. The man who shirks in some flagrant way often gets more severely dealt with than he deserves; he is thought a monster, or a hypocrite, when he is only a coward. Men whose general lives are creditable, — men who are leaders of opinion, who have weight in moral questions, who even take a lofty religious stand, who are avowedly not influenced by the point of honor, because they believe themselves exponents of a more spiritual rule, who are even ascetic both in notions and practice, — sometimes betray this craven impulse, to the confounding of their followers and admirers. Those are fortunate persons — but we will also add, of a limited experience — who can believe it simply impossible that a man whose head, heart, and hands seem to be habitually engaged in the highest concerns and interests, is disqualified from conspicuous acts of shirking. All people have their temptations. Men who are scrupulous to perform everything that comes to them as a religious duty will amaze their friends by some failure in matters of sentiment. Thus, we shall see a painstaking clergyman, who really works hard in his vocation, who preaches with unction, and of whom no one can say that he is not sincere and self-denying in his work, jilt the woman he has promised to marry; and he will do this, if he is matter-of-fact, with a perfectly obtuse complacency, simply because it is out of his professional line of duty, wherein all his scruples lie. Or, if he is of another temper, he will even think that the argument that marriage is too happy a state for such a sinner, or that some quality in the lady disables her from the companionship of an "earnest man," turns what the world regards as shirking in its worst sense into a spiritual sacrifice. All his tenderness of conscience goes with his office, and he shirks with the secular part of himself, and in what he is pleased to regard as secular, and therefore immaterial, concerns. Thus, getting out of an awkward engagement to marry is not very different from getting out of an inconvenient engagement to dinner, to a man who conceives himself lifted above the obligations of honor and custom.

Again, there are people who shirk nothing that comes to them in the way of work, however difficult, wearisome, or repulsive, who will yet shirk signally when interest, credit, popularity, or respect for a life's work, comes in the way. For such shirking we should, no doubt, have an especial indulgence, for the temptation is great. As a rule, for instance, Bishop Blomfield shirked nothing, — neither trouble, responsibility, nor irksome duty. His view of the duties of his position was indeed the widest ever known. It extended not only to the spiritual concerns of his diocese, but to the superintendence of its highways. He answered thirty letters a day by return of post, and how severely he was wont to express himself against all tendency to shirk and evasion we may gather by that letter to his publisher when ill, wherein he commands him to ascertain his real state "by a distinct and categorical appeal to his medical friends." Yet his memoir, as well as our own recollection, presents him to us, on the occasion of his famous charge, as one of the most signal cases of shirking that our age can furnish. But who shall be hard upon a man who fails under trial, when we all fail in our lesser spheres almost untempted! In fact, it is wandering from our first design to talk of bishops and popes and emperors. Our concern is with the social tendency, in all its infinite forms of manifestation. Every temperament has its natural and appropriate scene of slipperiness,—the idle, the busy, the sullen, the amiable, the selfish, and even the self-denying. Some shirk trouble, some responsibility, some bodily labor, some mental,—some the care of their health, some their accounts, some attention to dress and manners, some distinct obligations, some the demands of honor or gallantry, some recognized duties, some supposed pleasures. There is often something whimsical in the display of this evasive power. Thus, some are alive to the demands of personal intercourse who shirk writing an ordinary letter with an insane persistence; some are good at letters who cannot be brought to the sticking-point of writing a necessary note of ceremony; some who are austerely conscientious in what they own for obligations will slip out of an engagement to an irksome form of pleasure with an ease incomprehensible to the worldly man we have spoken of, who feels himself bound by his promise. Some who are liberal in great things will shirk small expenses with a ridiculous meanness; and some who are truth, strength, and honesty itself in all that concerns others, shirk for themselves, and are cowardly, weak, and treacherous in their own interest. There are men who cannot be brought up to the point where their own advancement or benefit is involved, and who, just at the last, are stranded and left behind by their inveterate habit of failing themselves and those who care for them, when the moment of action and decision comes. And there are lines of unconscious shirk where neither the man himself nor those who observe him use the word or see the thing. Where a man is not in the position in which his standing and powers ought to place him, and nobody knows why, failure is almost certainly due to a habit of small shirking, so constant and natural that it is never recognized for what it is.

There are, indeed, some people who surprise us by a sort of morbid dread of shirking, — stolid, helpess-seeming people, who accept duties that can hardly be called duties at all, and carry them on, not because they like them or value themselves upon doing them, or from any conscious sense of duty, but because they do not seem to know how to shirk them. They go on with a task that does not belong to them, because, though they cannot argue or reason upon it, they have a constitutional dislike, contempt, or perhaps simple incapacity for shirking in this particular direction. A great amount of the good works done are carried on by this unpretending, unconscious sort of virtue, — virtue that plods and drudges, and does not know itself for what it is. Yet we should always fear to infuse into these good souls the perilous and insidious delight of waking to a way of escape from what before seemed inevitable; for who can tell to what limits the new sensation would confine itself? It is so pleasant, such a relief, it induces often such a calm, to discover that, after all, we need not do a thing which we had thought before must be done, because in strict fantastical right it ought. The possibility of shirking, in prospect at least, never occurs to some people at all, while it occurs to others at the very first blush. They accept a duty, a promise, a responsibility, tempered by the possibility of shirking it. Thus the sin of shirking dates from before the act. The man who undertakes an engagement, and subsequently shirks it, has never been firm; he has always had a vague notion that there are two ways out of it.

Small shirks may be apples of Sodom, but they clearly constitute with some people one of the main pleasures of life. Ease in the abstract is a thing scarcely understood. To sit loose from minor obligations, to feel unfettered by the ties of implied promises or the expectation of others, gives ease a body, and makes it intelligible and practical. But it is better that this should be an unconscious gloss of the word; it is better, even if we shirk, that we should be in a measure blind to it. It becomes serious when the confession of shirking costs us nothing, for it imperils one safeguard of our honor. No one who shirks, and knows it, and jauntily owns it, can be sure of confining himself to the range of lesser and immaterial shirkings. However, this is a temptation only of the careless, indolent temper. Busy men, when they shirk, call it expediency, and defend it as such.

We have admitted that shirking is pleasant, and people who shirk in a small way are often very lovable people, and we are comfortable, careless, and at ease in their company. Yet many of the difficulties and estrangements of life proceed from it, — from evading some insignificant, trifling, social duty that would cost a very slight effort, but is shirked as a momentary nuisance; and once call a gentle obligation by a bad name, — a nuisance or a bore, — and your real shirker considers himself absolved. If he is fortunate in having some one, — a wife, a friend, a slave, — to do his hard work, and sweep up the litter of broken promises after him, it is well, — so much is excused to pleasant people; but he is not the less an element of dissolution. Loose himself, nothing will knit firmly about him; and every one who evades an obvious social duty because it is disagreeable and he would rather not, is, however professedly conservative, promoting disunion and weakening the social fabric.

CONSTANCY.

CONSTANCY is not the undisputed virtue that it used to be. To be faithful to an idea, to hold by a choice once made, to cling with unflinching tenacity to the object of past vows and promises under every conceivable form of trial, was, to say the least, meritorious. Under the poets' and romancers' hands, it was sublime. Some change has certainly come over this view. Constancy, in common parlance, still holds its place among the virtues, yet we observe a decided tendency to shackle it with restrictions and conditions, and somewhat to flout it, in what may be called its raw state, as an unreasoning, blind instinct. The necessities of our times enforce some modification. All ages have their easy and their difficult virtues; and in an active, thinking, changeful, busy scene, constancy is often so difficult, and involves such conflicts between qualities good in themselves, that we do not wonder that those who find the traditional grace press hardest are sometimes disposed to call it in question. Perhaps, if we think of it, constancy has always been of two sexes, — the masculine and reasonable, where a man chooses his cause as embodying his ideas of highest good and stands to it as such; the feminine and instinctive, which holds with a fixed, unswerving faith to a choice once made, as being best because it was her choice, not her choice because it is best. And it is this form, imposing as it were upon the weaker vessel, that poets have sung and woman once gladly owned to; but these days of enlightenment seem to have awakened her to another view of the subject, or rather those bolder spirits who put themselves forward as exponents of their sex's true position. Two popular novelists of the day may be said to represent the two sides of this question of romantic constancy. Mr. Trollope is all for constancy, thoroughgoing, immovable, blind. In the "Three Clerks," his heroine, between her two lovers, makes the wrong choice. Her husband goes to the bad, is convicted of felony, and expiates his crime, no humiliation being spared, in Millbank Prison; but throughout she is constant, not only in act, but in idea; her husband is still of a type quite superior to, and more heroic than, that which belongs to her virtuous and discarded lover. Again, in a later tale, the too confiding and demonstrative Lily is jilted by Crosbie under the most inexcusable and scandalous circumstances; but she will not hear a word against him, shrinks from blaming him to herself, and has the praise of constancy. The authoress of "Adam Bede," in "Romola," — that studied, thoughtful, well-written, hard-to-read story, — asserts another principle altogether. The moral of the tale is, that wives must not go on loving bad husbands, that they must not shrink from seeing things exactly as they are, or from regulating heart and conduct by their conclusions. It goes so far as to deny that the affections are under any obligation irrespective of merit, or that there is any moral force even in the marriage tie where one side shows itself unworthy, — in this only following at a distance the teaching of certain strong-minded Transatlantic ladies, who have dauntlessly struck at the very root of all constancy by their theory that no decisions, no choice, no professions, vows, or ties whatever, can ever alienate the right of being attracted by the highest representative of the ideal that crosses our path. At present, they say, "a mistaken education, a narrow, uncultivated mind, and many prejudices, tend to make women more constant than men"; but when once woman realizes that she has a "range," this spiritless dependence must come to an end, as entirely opposed to individual progress and loftiness of aim. Constancy then is put upon its trial, and has to defend itself against some very plausible objections. Why may we not go on forever choosing the best in every sphere of life and thought, and discarding what has failed to satisfy this intellectual desire? Why did the poet think he had hit upon a blot in poor nature, rather than an excellence, when he proves it unstable? —

> "Opinions, they still take a wider range;
> Find, if you can, in what you cannot change.
> Manners with fortune, humors turn with climes,
> Tenets with books, and principles with times."

We have taken the popular field for the exhibition of constancy, — constancy in love, not because this is the main or necessarily the most distinctive sphere for its exercise, but because it presents the circumstances necessary for a picture of constancy at all. A plighted troth implies, in our understanding of it, a deliberate act in both parties, a mutual surrender of heart and affections, an engagement and a covenant; and constancy in every sphere requires for its exercise the deliberate, willing act of a mind, competent to perform such an act, as its commencement. People are often called inconstant to whom the accusation is totally inapplicable. There is no such thing as inconstancy where there has been no starting-point of selection and decision. A man is not inconstant for deserting the family politics to which he was committed before he had fit opportunities for bringing his own mind to bear upon them. He is not inconstant in forsaking his father's friends, to whom experience proves him not congenial. The fault, where there is a fault, should go by some other name. He is ungrateful, perhaps, for kindness; or he has been rash in committing himself, or he is misled by ambition and vanity.

Thus constancy is, first of all, truth to self, and implies standing by our own judgment, as well as by our friend; and the worth of this posture of mind must, in a good degree, depend on the nature of the original act, whether founded on reason and desert in the object, or on mere caprice, or for selfish ends. In the question of opinion, a boy may elect to be Whig or Tory from the love of freedom on the one hand, or from chivalrous loyalty on the other; and, noble associations adding strength day by day to the original bias, he may be constant to the party which in his mind embodies one or other of these ideas. Or he may choose his politics by a lower scale of preferences altogether, and in this case no length or tenacity of tenure can make low principles of action more respectable. If there was no sense or judgment in the first choice, mere obstinacy in abiding by it cannot be meritorious, though it is often flattered and over-valued as being something to be relied upon. What passes for constancy is generally mere habit, and individuals and classes are constant or not, as this habit has undisturbed means of growth. In youth, constancy seems the simplest and easiest thing in the world, and where — as providentially in the marriage relation — men are secure from change and opposing interest, it is so. It is natural. Constancy is, in fact, the rule, and inconstancy the exception. But the constancy worth commending maintains itself under difficulties, and especially against that great rival force in every vigorous mind, — susceptibility to new impressions. Some people's constancy, or what they claim as such, is mere stupidity and deadness to what ought to interest and attract them. They stand among facts that ought to open their eyes, and persons that ought to engage their affections, and are proud of the apathy and prejudice that makes them "like old ways and old friends best." Now the truth is, every healthy mind is occupied mainly with the present and what the present gives it to do. While the house is in repair, it entertains a perpetual succession of guests, and echoes to new voices; it is only ruins that are constant, in this sense, to memories and unchanging ideas. Active, living constancy recognizes the inevitable workings of change. It is absurd to suppose of a soul that is to last forever, that its thoughts and affections should be limited to the interests of a particular period, or a few individuals. As we live, we change, — change ourselves, and change in our relation to others; and the more stationary friend often calls this inconstancy. Inexperience cannot believe in the inevitable results of new combinations and altered circumstances. Indeed, nature could not endure to stand among the keenly felt interests that surround our youth, — the friends, the pursuits, the tastes, the controversies, the whole world's course, — and be forced to realize how, in thirty, twenty, nay, ten years, all these things will have lost their likeness to us and we to them; and yet this is inevitable where people do a work in the world and make their existence felt. Now the thing is, to be constant under what in prospect looks like inconstancy, to acknowledge change, and adapt ourselves to it, but to hold by one original starting-point, and be faithful to the one idea and the one friend through it all. To bring about this there must have been a different view of the object of regard from the first. The constant mind need not have exceptional strength of character, but it must have what is often a much finer thing, — an independent judgment and generous self-reliance. It must have been guided in its first choice by its own unprompted act and deed, and be able to maintain it against opposing influences, not by ignoring those influences, but by asserting the old preference against them. Constancy, grand, heroic, and exemplary, then, must always be a rare quality, — as rare, that is, as independence of mind, which is about the most unusual quality we any of us meet with.

However, the praise of constancy may be bestowed on individuals short of this heroic stature, though never where self-reliance is wanting; and these sometimes furnish us with curious opportunities for inspecting the mechanism of this virtue. We are disposed to think that with this quality, with fidelity in views, in friendship, and affection, there goes a strong sense of possession, a raised appreciation of any property whatever where the notion of proprietorship can be applied to it. Thus the words, or at least the idea, of My and Mine have a particular value and importance with this temper; they warp the judgment, and add a certain percentage to everything that can be so appropriated. Who is not familiar with some artless example of faithfulness to old impressions, — some good, enduring soul who has never lost a friend through fault or negligence, whose memory ranges through a life of well-hoarded friendships as deep as the character is capable of forming, whose conversation is a kindly chronicle of reciprocal services? We will venture something that this personage—we will assume her to be of the gentler sex—will be hampered by a vast number of small possessions, trifling in themselves, but invested in her eyes with a factitious importance, partly from sentiment and association, but also because they are her own. We have observed persons of this sort with a trick of, as it were, taking stock and making sure of their appendages by little searchings and fumblings, under sudden accesses of alarm lest chain, or brooch, or reticule should have unloosed their moorings, and made off unto that terror of the constant heart, the unseen and forgotten; and it has occurred to us, whether this little scene may not set out to us some similar practice of the mind towards friends and allies, and represent thought ever busied, with canine instinct, in looking up stragglers in the band of intimates, devising letters, messages, and other kindly remembrances, and enduring, forbearing, tolerating, excusing all those waverers who, if left to themselves, and under most people's handling, would be permanent defaulters from the flock. Persons of this sort—dependable friends—do not lose their sticks and umbrellas like other people, because they have a distinct notion where they put them. Their sense of personality extends to watch, and pencil, and books. They will lend liberally, but they always know who has the missing volume.

Very different notions, we are aware, are current. It may even be supposed that the cares of friendship make a man forgetful of the merely personal; and people may make grand spasmodic sacrifices who are of the careless, lavish, prodigal turn, apt to be seized with a sudden indifference to their belongings; but both parties in a friendship must be endowed with an unusual constancy of nature to maintain it without flaw or damage under the rude trial of large obligations; and a weighty favor conferred without counting the cost is usually fatal to it. We would gladly think that our friend values us as one of his possessions, and is careful of us on the same grounds; and if, for our sake, he should ever endanger money or credit or popularity, that he will do it, not rashly or thoughtlessly, but knowing it to be a sacrifice. People not exactly miserly, but mean and narrow in their notions about money, often surprise us by a certain exceptional fidelity towards old friends. In this case, their constancy is probably not of a very noble order. The general restriction of their ideas preserves them from the temptations which ambition or imagination opens to larger minds; but if it modifies the value of their regard on the one hand, it redeems their love of money for its own sake from some of its baseness. It is not rapacity, but a perverted sense of ownership, — that ownership which makes the steady mind value its possessions, and exaggerate the worth of all that is its own. Perhaps, indeed, it is only the larger and higher constancy that can afford to be critical. A just perception of faults and blemishes hidden from their possessors is the cause of a good deal of the inconstancy that gets called the hardest names. True constancy can see and yet be faithful, but often at an unknown expense. The good people who more commonly represent the quality are full of favorable prejudices, and see the merits of their cause or their friend with quite different eyes from their defects. We should augur ill for Touchstone's constancy, even if he himself had betrayed no suspicions, because he saw Audrey exactly as she was, — "A poor thing, but mine own." He had the sense of possession, but he regarded her with too critical an eye, or rather, which is more fatal still, with the eye of the critic to whom he introduced her. It is a great step towards security when our friend is proud of us.

If constancy is what we believe it to be, a moral virtue, it may be acquired in spite of every natural tendency to fickleness and change. A due training of the temper and disposition may bring a mind, which at first only resembles the mirror in reflecting every image that flits across it, into a surface capable of receiving lasting impressions. Yet there must be no conscious effort in constancy; it must not be confounded with duty, which often, with much labor and pains, has to do its work. A man may, indeed, be worthily constant in an unworthy cause; but if the sentiment deserves the name, he has lived, and still lives, under a delusion. If he once sees the worthlessness of an object, constancy is not the proper epithet for his loyalty to it; it is then either duty or infatuation. The tie between the first choice and the present estimate is severed, and it is regarded from a wholly different point of view. If he has promised love and service to the end, and thinks constancy a virtue, he will act it out in deed if not in thought; and habit even here will assert itself a second nature, and help and cheer him through the hardest task. If, on the contrary, he takes the transcendental view that he has passed out of the sphere of the old love, he may, whether the object of past regard be deserving or not, content himself with curiously noting the transitions of feeling; apostrophizing it in the words of a distinguished and popular authoress, who has lately been so obliging as to tell us how inconstancy feels in its first workings: "O dead root of love! who shall tell the mystery of your nipping? How, with startled eyes, suddenly we miss the colored blossoms and fresh green leaves that should be there!" Inconstancy, no doubt, comes of false and unreasonable expectations, an intolerance of the levels and barren spaces, the checks and inequalities of the pleasantest intercourse, a demand for change and variety which one mind or one state of things will not furnish. "Even tempers and uniform dispositions" are prepared for this, and those who have the doubtful praise of "being always the same" recognize no difficulty; but wherever there is the charm of quick, eager sensibilities, a lively imagination, and a fastidiously delicate perception, there we must be indulgent to a tendency to caprice and disgust, there we must be prepared, on our part, for what seems to us an undue share of endurance, — there we must put our own constancy on the stretch, if we would not indulge the world with the scandal of a broken friendship or a deserted cause. Our duties to others ought to be continually looked at from their point of view. Appearances are sometimes the heart of things, and, in critical tests of constancy, must often be so. There is a rule which we think would make all men constant, whatever their natural bias; and this is, in trifling services, as in great things, never willingly to disappoint a just and reasonable expectation.

RESERVE.

RESERVE, as denoting a characteristic, is, comparatively speaking, a new word. Old writers now and then call a man reserved, coupling the idea with policy or constitutional melancholy; but the word reserve, as meaning an innate quality of a healthy mind, we do not meet with. In fact there was not, in other days, the occasion for it which we find among ourselves. Reserve was not a national quality, as it is supposed to be now; and if people wanted to attribute something of the kind to their acquaintance, they commonly expressed their meaning by some harsher term, — sour perhaps, morose, sullen, proud, lofty, taciturn, or dissembling. Or the objectionable trait was summarily set down to "humors," and a thickness of the blood. That a man should lead a shut-up life, should deliberately conceal the best part of himself, his more intimate and individual sentiments, from the society of which he forms a part, — and that this habit of his should affect others with admiration, and with a raised and excited expectation, does not accord with the way of thinking of those less fastidious times when wits talked their very best in coffee-houses or other public resorts, and were very willing to let who would hear them. There was little of what we understand by reserve in days when probably every one's arena for bringing out what was in him was found in mixed companies or casual intercourse, not in the close feminine domestic circle of modern refinement, nor in the habitual exclusive intercourse of one or two chosen intimates who can be relied upon for understanding every turn of thought and shade of feeling.

Whatever our fathers did, it is a word that we, at least, could ill spare, — "reserve" accounts for and explains so many things. And yet what that reserve is which is not pride, nor sullenness, nor shyness, nor dulness, nor melancholy, nor affectation, but a thing altogether apart from all these, is not so easy to define. The first social example of the quality that occurs to us is the poet Gray, and it is amusing to see how the old rough frankness bristled and clashed against the new exclusive element. It is very little to Johnson's credit that he did not admire Gray's poetry, but Johnson was a conservative, and Gray was in all things a precursor and innovator. Thus, he started the popular love of the picturesque, and is the first solitary tourist on record. He wrote poetry that men vowed they could not understand, just as old-fashioned folks do now by "In Memoriam." He set up, and acted on, a new theory of social and literary independence; and he was reserved, — reserved in the new heroic way: that is, he had a vast number of contempts and antipathies, and some warm friendships; he mistrusted mankind, but where he gave his confidence it was unlimited; he loved but one woman, and she was his mother, but this love was pathetic and exemplary; and, finally, he shut himself up and eschewed general society. This was not the character to suit Johnson's old-world practice or principles, and he summarily disposed of it after his manner. "Sir, he was a dull fellow, — dull in company, dull in his closet, dull everywhere; he was dull in a new way, and that made many people think him great." Now the poet, in his own line, was great, and to his intimates was, and deserved to be, pre-eminently interesting; but we believe this is a fair enough picture of his actual deportment to the world at large. And reserve is dulness to the majority of those who come in contact with it, — a fact which it may not be amiss to press at a time when everybody is pleased to be thought reserved, and disowns the charge with the gentlest disclaimer, either for his country or himself.

There is a reserve merely of manner, of which we will only say that it is much to be preferred to the opposite extreme; but reserve of mind — the attitude of holding back what is most distinctive of the speaker, and what affects him nearest — disqualifies a man for general cheerful companionship. Not that we would confound reserve with dulness. A practised observer distinguishes the two before a word is spoken. As Bacon says, "If a man be thought secret, it inviteth discovery," which dulness never does. In reserve there is, for those who care for such things, the interest of detecting the real man through the veil it pleases him to wear. The character most liable to it has high and attractive points, — it has self-respect, self-restraint, sensitiveness, and possibly a high moral standard and a correct taste; but the reserve itself, if not an innate fault, is yet a misfortune. It is the effect of some early check, neglect, wounded feeling, or uncongenial circumstances when the character began to form itself. And it results in harm; for that must be a narrowing, if not a hardening quality which keeps a man always on the defensive, and suspicious of aggression, and shuts him up from real, equal, open intercourse with the greater number of those who fall in his way. It is no credit to a man that very few people know him, and yet it is constantly stated by his friends as a sort of distinction separating him from the common herd, who lay themselves bare — thoughts, feelings, emotions — at the mere prompting of the occasion, without jealous choice of witnesses or care for a fit audience.

It is sometimes thought a sign of freedom from egotism that a man never speaks of himself; but it more commonly denotes reserve, and is, in truth, one of its more repelling characteristics. Reserve is compatible with great freedom and fluency of speech on those subjects which are public property. Indeed, men who are conscious that they hold an impregnable position are often very ready on common topics, and may even conceal from the unobservant that there is a part of themselves which no eye is ever permitted to pry into. But this sort of talk, in the long run, is unsatisfactory, — it wants the savor of candor and true sincerity. The reserved and the open are not even here on a level, for there is no subject so removed from personal interests and regards as not to suffer in the handling from this watchful jealousy lest the general should touch on the private and individual. Whatever a man is, however attractive his powers or qualities, if he persistently shuns personal confidences where it would be natural to make them, it is wise to accept the reticence as a sign of mistrust. Acquaintance here will not ripen into friendship. All people, we may be sure, talk of themselves to somebody, and it is, in fact, an especial luxury to the reserved class, from their self-inverted, self-conscious habit of mind. This sometimes impels them to strange confidences. A man of rigid reserve will tell a stranger things about himself which he has hid from friend, and wife, and child; and this either from a grudging mistrust of those near him, — lest the barrier, once broken down, should never be raised again, — or because he can talk of things the most intimate and close to him if secure from the free, bold touch of sympathy and affection. Thus it is that confiding, cordial natures are often invaded with something like a pang, as at kindness repelled and interest slighted, when they find that their reserved friend has been revealing his inner nature to a chance talkative stranger, which he has withheld from them through long seeming intimacy, interchange of kind offices, and tried fidelity. In fact, when frank and friendly people call a man reserved, it commonly means some personal experience of this sort.

It is, perhaps, impossible not to be flattered by anything like exclusive regard. We are all so far selfish as to prize a thing the more for its being, in some particular sense, our own: —

> "And what alone did all the rest surpass,
> The sweet possession of the fairy place;

> Single, and conscious to myself alone
> Of pleasures to the excluded world unknown."

And here, no doubt, lies much of the charm of reserve, — it points to something which may become an exclusive possession. Nor do some persons care how narrow is the outlet for sensibility and enthusiasm, so that it flows freely for them. If a man does not open his heart to many people, he is too readily assumed to be capable of a particular effusion and intensity of trust in a chosen few. The truth is, however, that nothing really needs such constant practice as the affections. A man does not feel a bit the stronger for feeling rarely; and we would go further, and say that the man who resolutely controls all expression of feeling controls something more than expression, — he keeps down the thing itself. An exclusive manner cannot be maintained without a certain cast of sentiment toward the persons against whom this guard is kept. The outside does not belie the heart, as is fondly supposed; it more commonly understates the real condition of affairs. And yet, because all silence and reticence have an air of mystery, we often see the frank genial nature — which, like the green fields, bears its wealth visible to all eyes — disregarded for one of these supposed mines of treasure and centres of hidden fire. It is woman's weakness especially to be caught by the romance of a stern, inaccessible nature, accessible to her and to her alone, — more particularly if she be of the jealous temper which grudges sharers in its privileges. Reserve gives great occasion for her particular talent of practical physiognomy. If the countenance is impenetrable, then

> "Calm pleasures there abide, majestic pains";

if rigid, she can detect lightning flashes of feeling; if mobile, and subject to transitions and rapid fluctuations of expression, it is like a map of a country of which she alone has the key. What depths of tenderness, humanity, and intellect will she not attribute to eyes that kindle while the tongue is mute, to a brow that contracts under unexpressed thought, and to lips that pass from stern to sweet under restrained impulses! Yet mere sensitiveness — sensitiveness that never gets wholly away from self, never quite loses itself in others — may be at the bottom of the simulating exterior. The shyness of pride, the horror of self-betrayal, the fear of ridicule, or the intense enjoyment and appreciation of being understood, are all very tell-tale emotions, and can dispense with speech. Where reserve is a strong characteristic, even thoughts of universal kindliness are no habitual occupation of heart or intellect; though the want may be more than atoned for to the favored few by a warm partiality of preference, confiding dependence, and depth of personal regard. Where there is this harmony, let the union be as close and as exclusive as it will. Reserve is an element of strength, and has its work to do in the world as a check on babbling sentiment and on the weak effusions of shallow or boisterous natures. We do not care to have everybody diffusively and expansively benevolent. What we resent is the waste that is sometimes observable of an honest regard, — a confidence on one side, with efforts to please that are not, and never will be, returned. We find something lowering in some people's humble attendance on tempers of this nature, — in their waiting and watching for chance crumbs of sympathy. There is always a time when these unrequited endeavors should cease. Sympathy and confidence should be mutual, or they should tone down to a lower level. A lover was once refused, at the end of fifteen years, on the ground of insufficient acquaintance. It is wise in friend as well as suitor to give up the hope of occupying any large place in the mind which has had ample opportunities of knowing all the good that is in him, and yet has not availed itself of them.

A certain set of strong qualities can hardly be found in man without the counterbalance of contempt and disdain. Being free from a particular class of temptations, people despise those who are subject to them. Above all, the power of silence is one to be proud of, both for the snares and dangers from which it saves, and the prestige which it wins. All reserved people have mistrust of others. Most of them undervalue the discretion or refinement of those among whom they live. It is almost necessarily a supercilious habit of mind, and this is apparent whenever a man of reserved temper will talk frankly of his reserve. He owns that the mass of mankind are beyond — which means beneath — his sympathy. He will confess to being hopeless — which, again, means careless — of their regard. There may, indeed, be the appearance of reserve from opposite causes, — from the mere want of a sense of individuality. Some people have no privacy because their own nature never occupies them. They cannot be brought to talk about themselves, or to make confidences, from mere ignorance of the subject. Their fault is an intellectual one, and the less need be said about them because they are essentially dry and uninteresting. Nobody cares much what they may have to say on any topic, and their reserve is what only the more philanthropic would seek to break through.

Shyness and reserve are so often alike in their effects that it is no wonder they are constantly confounded. Shyness, under a composed exterior, looks like reserve; and reserve, where people judge only by manner, often passes for shyness. But the likeness is only superficial. It is easy to distinguish, where there is opportunity for observation, the painful shrinking and recoil which puts Shyness at a distance, from the arm's-length attitude of resistance by which Reserve holds the world at bay. Genuine shyness must be some compound of fear, self-consciousness, and inexperience. It implies an acute sense of bareness and exposure, which intercourse with the world will certainly modify. What reserve is, we have not arrived at; but it is a quality, when once implanted, which custom and society will rather increase than wear out. It is felt to be a power and a protection, and is cherished as an armor of defence; and so it is, but it is also an admission of weakness and an evidence of defect. With all respect and liking too for our reserved friends, and for the impressive appearance which a well-guarded reserve makes in the world, we yet submit that the strongest minds, — the most vigorous, comprehensive, prudent, and far-seeing, the natures most to be relied upon, most influential, and most thoroughly amiable, — are essentially unreserved.

EXPLANATIONS.

THERE are few words that carry a heavier weight of dulness, or are beset with more annoying associations than "Explanation," and the verb "To Explain," in all its tenses. We do not remember that the poets give them a place in the armory of Discord; but, in their dull, hypocritical way, none deserve it better, for every so-called explanation induces some element of discordance and separation, and puts the speaker in a sort of opposition of sentiment or inclination to the hearer. The words have, no doubt, an innocent use as applied to things; but when men come to explain a meaning that had previously seemed too clear, or to give an explanation of a questionable course of conduct, or to seek an explanation of a line of action which has displeased them, — above all, when, under the privilege of intimacy, there is a mutual unfolding of motives and intentions with the professed design of explaining away some chance coldness or difference, — it is rare that mischief does not come of it. And as for truth, which is the professed aim, who was ever thoroughly satisfied with himself, whose conscience ever came out quite white and clean, after some tooth-and-nail explanation on some intricate knotty point in which his feelings or passions have been engaged? The sense of failure after these encounters is, indeed, so general that we believe the practice would be about given up by rational people but for a perversion of language which universally prevails. Wherever neighbors and acquaintances do not quite hit it, wherever there is some slight breach or halt in intimacy, the state of things is called a misunderstanding. The affair is politely attributed to the respective parties not knowing enough of each other's inner motives and opinions, — it being assumed that the more people know exactly what goes on inside each other, the greater friends they will be. Now, of course, if ignorance lies at the bottom of the difficulty, an explanation has some chance of removing it; and thus, the word "misunderstanding" suggests naturally the idea of explaining it away. But if misunderstanding, as we believe, always means collision, the recourse to explanation is manifestly absurd; and that the word does convey this meaning, those at least will not doubt who have, on the other hypothesis, tried what an elaborate explanation of themselves can do. Pure untinctured mistake has not much to do with human affairs out of novels. In fact, all minds brought into near contact are aware, except where the ties of a lifelong family affection and unity of interests blind them, of certain incongruous elements and points of antagonism which untoward circumstances occasionally bring into prominence. There is some quality in each unit of the most attached pair of friends, or even lovers, which is not acceptable or agreeable to the other, — which, when uppermost, causes a rub, and results even in a sense of mutual blame, — but which need not cause any lasting disturbance if recognized for what it is, an inborn difference or defect, a spot come into sight. For collisions are passing things, — even serious collisions; if we weather the first shock, we may go on as before, merely learning a scarcely conscious lesson of caution. But in impulsive minds a desire arises to do something. Self has to be cleared, or another has to be called to account; we must needs get at the bottom of things, and see where the fault lies, and once for all make things straight. Now, whenever this craving arises, the friendship or familiarity has arrived at one of its inevitable hitches; and it is certainly wisest to go round it, if possible, — not to make too violent efforts to remove what is deeper rooted and harder to shift than haste and inexperience will believe. Clashes of feeling or opinion must come, sooner or later, when there are hidden differences. The warmest friendship must be content with something short of absolute unanimity, — must now and then endure tacit disapproval, must rely on a general estimate of conduct, must submit to be what it calls mistaken, while in reality there is as good an understanding as innate differences and opposing views and interests will allow.

Few persons are aware how seldom they act in the affairs of life on a formal array of reasons. All people who are fond of explanations have more than half their reasons to seek on the spur of the moment and in the heat of talk. In fact, men act on the principles that have formed their characters, but very seldom think of reasons till after an affair is over. Hence all sorts of temptations to be disingenuous. The mind must be very candid and transparent which comes out of one of these explanatory duels unconscious of suppressions and special pleadings, and of glosses which a man may be sure his opponent has seen more clearly than himself, and which may unduly lower his opinion of his sincerity. When the Frenchwoman explained that she wished for a divorce because she could practise no virtue with the Dutchman, nobody would give her credit for the particle of truth which was possibly there. To persons who cannot follow the causes of your conduct intuitively, your reasons evoked at a moment's notice are not likely to make matters better, or better understood; for a reason which barely represents half your motives to yourself is sure to enter the other mind in such travestied guise as to convey nothing as you intend it. A man's principles may be good, and the application of them nothing to be ashamed of, but he has found them hardly presentable without a little varnish. In fact, motives of conduct are such complex things that they often refuse to be put into words. In private and individual cases, moreover, they may have no possible disgrace in them, and yet there may be a pardonable reluctance to proclaim them. Self-respect and want of appropriate language drive people in these predicaments to the hypocrisy of a higher ground than they have a right to. Sydney Smith, arguing with "a good honest Tory" on Catholic Emancipation, asks of what importance it is to him whether a Protestant or Catholic is made a judge? "None," is the disinterested answer; "but I am afraid for the Church of Ireland." "Why do you care so much for the Church of Ireland?" "I do not care so much for the Church of Ireland, if I were sure the Church of England would not be destroyed." "And is it for the Church of

England alone that you fear?" is the insinuating rejoinder. "Not quite that," comes out at last, "but I am afraid we should all be lost, — that everything would be overturned, and that I should lose my rank and my estate." In politics, a party may be made to explain itself in this fashion, — may be driven to a confession of selfish as well as public ends, without leaving a soreness behind; but there are a hundred private motives and considerations in social life which will not bear such treatment, and which cannot be forced into words and made distinctly visible without a sense of humiliation, and yet which are quite as lawful as the Tory's regard for his own estate.

Conversation and all social intercourse are carried on under the notion of a certain masonic comprehension more subtle than language, and nothing is so embarrassing to our candor and sense of truth as to find this freemasonry at fault. Families, cliques, societies, understand one another with this electric rapidity; but wherever temper or opposing interests break the mystic link, friends and intimates are in the position of opposing classes, who have to lay down everything in the way of formal explanation. Words are powerless to restore the old flash of recognition, and it is very seldom wise to have recourse to them, where there are such hinderances on each side as impeded sympathies, and perception blinded by eager self-vindication.

People, indeed, who have faith in explanations and periodical repairs of their friendships, had need of an exceptional amount of charity, or of some Lethe of their own wherein to bathe their memory after them; for we are comparatively indifferent to being misunderstood, or even misjudged, where it comes of our friend's blunder, or his dulness to our merits, but nobody can stand having his array of statements, his proofs, arguments, justifications, set at naught. It is intolerable, after condescending to a laborious vindication, to remain where we were,—after an unanswerable display of grievances, to see our friend unconvinced and impenitent; and yet some touch of this evil clings to every explanation, with whatever temper conducted. But what temper can come wholly unscathed out of the ordeal? In many hands, explanations, of course, slip at once into mere recrimination, proceeding to the scandal of a quarrel and mutual loss of respect, even where reconciliation ensues. But short of this, and where principle, self-control, and politeness are never lost sight of, this form of encounter brings out many awkward revelations. Few natures ring true through their whole depths. There is a savage, untamed spot in most hearts. Education and the discipline of society do not subdue the whole man. We do not slander humanity in saying that few men are gentlemen under every conceivable trial. Something rough and rude lurks, unknown, unseen, in many an elegant, refined bosom, civilized by all that culture can do, and proof against all attacks recognized as such, but which reveals itself under the insidious temptation of one of these friendly passages at arms. Of all possible forms of this evil, the worst and the most dangerous is where members of the same household or family, ceasing to trust to instinct and experience, in their perilous intimacy throw themselves upon verbal explanations.

It may be observed, that the people who keep their friends, and live in a state of harmony with the world, systematically deny themselves the luxury of explanations. Things go a little wrong, but they wait patiently until they right themselves. They trust to time, to patience, to the weight of a composed and forbearing attitude, to the powerful influences of reticence and self-respect. While people are much and variously involved in the world's business and pleasures, they hardly recognize the temptation to this undignified form of exculpatory vindication and self-assertion. Indeed, a fondness for explanations can scarcely possess persons in the brisk intercourse of life. It demands time to brood. It belongs to pauses in the hurry of existence, — to the byways of life. Women are more given to it than men; dwellers in small towns than in great. Even the same people take to explanations in the country which they would never think of making in London. Apart from any sense of neglect or grievance, there is a constant tendency in some minds to explain themselves and right themselves in the eyes of the world. All people who do not come up to their own idea of themselves, and are afflicted with morbid misgivings that they do not do themselves justice, have this habit. A person of this sort will plunge into any depth of new blunder in explaining away his last solecism. It is, in fact, the way conceit works where it has rare occasions for display and wants a field. Most people's consciousness will tell them that, if ever a fit of explaining themselves has been upon them, it has been in some flutter of self-love, self-consciousness, or self-interest. This at once differs from, and is more pardonable than, that solemn sense of importance which impels some men to explain every step in their course of action, — to give a reason for everything they do, under the notion that they are examples. There are dull prosers whose lips are engaged all their lives in a running comment on their actions, — who, like Mr. Collins, cannot take a hand at whist without detaining their hostess to explain why they think such a step justifiable and becoming to their position. Poor people are very prone to obtrude tedious apologetic explanations on their betters, sometimes to the suspension of all rational talk,—not from conceit, but from an inevitable ignorance of the small hold which their chance ceremonial intercourse has on persons remote from their ways of thought, and full of other things. Nor does all their desire to be civil preserve them from the common fate of explanations where self is necessarily prominent; as where the rustic, eager to atone for some fancied want of respect to a stranger at the Hall, opens his apology, on next meeting the distinguished visitor, with—"I 'm sure, sir, if I 'd had the least notion as you was a gentleman—" But, indeed, in less clumsy hands, it needs the greatest tact to enter on an affair of this kind without making worse of it; and, generally, to explain the why and because of a failure in respect or appreciation is only to commit a fresh and more offensive blunder, and is not seldom taken for deliberate impertinence. It may be noted that persons who have the art of managing others never explain themselves. To give reasons for a course of conduct is at once to expose it to criticism, and to deprive it of the weight which belongs to action as the result of character. The "Times," for instance, is as careful never to explain itself as it is never to apologize. Indeed, it may be doubted whether the most powerful and influential wills ever explain reasons or probe into motives, even to themselves. They have an instinct of working their way and effecting their purposes, which is the exact contrary of the bore's state of mind, — the man who influences nobody, — whom we have represented as always employed in explaining to himself and other people why he does things.

We started with the admission that some explanations are both innocent and necessary. Children are entrapped, as it were, by their trick of questioning, into the trial of listening to formal explanations in answer. Some things must be learnt by this method, however little "sympathy it has with the will of man." Not seldom we have seen a careless talker betray himself into the same snare, and writhe under the penance which, through nobody's fault but his own, he has brought upon himself. But we maintain that orators, teachers, conversers, should, one and all, be chary of the explanatory form, as being apt in its nature not only to induce tedium in the listener, but a sort of dogged resistance. Thus, between two preachers of equal power, the question of popularity will be decided by the mode in which their teaching is administered. The man who explains tires his hearers. The man who makes statements interests them. The demand on the attention in his case is less arbitrary, and it is given with less effort. In the one case, a man seems full of his subject, — in the other, of his own way of putting it; and while there may not seem much in common between the "explanations" of social life and the didactic explanation of the teacher, there is this likeness, — that the person engaged upon either of them is putting his case in his own point of view, and requiring us to see with his eyes.

HUGGER-MUGGER.

MOST minds have an untidy corner. Most men have a taste, in some quarter or other, for hugger-mugger, — for unworthy shifts and expedients, or for mere slovenliness and its musty comforts. Where circumstances run absolutely counter to this tendency, and will allow it no natural indulgence, it sometimes becomes a craving of the soul for shabbiness and squalor. Thus we read of kings casting off their robes of state to don greasy dressing-gowns, to shuffle about in old slippers, to recreate themselves in occupations whose charm lies in grimy shirt-sleeves and blackened hands. We are told of quondam beauties who have indemnified themselves for the pains of vanity, the restraints of slim waists and tortured locks, buckram, brocade, and diamonds, by a soily, snuffy old age; and of little princes kicking and screaming to be allowed to play in the mud of the streets. We do not, however, pretend that this passion for hugger-mugger is common. It is, rather, a lurking kindness in most of us, showing itself sometimes in mere trivial eccentricities, sometimes as a sort of necessary set-off to a great deal of pretension, — an economy in small things to atone for a great extravagance. Thus the taste for show is more commonly than not qualified by a secret fancy for hugger-mugger; not really because it is cheap, though perhaps this imposture is maintained, but because there is in most people a divided allegiance towards themselves. They like the world to take a certain exalted view of them and their pretensions, while they have an inner consciousness that they have no real claim to this position. When you reach their innermost notion of what is due to them, it comes to this, that anything will do; and there is a positive satisfaction in making anything do, provided nobody else knows or sees. No doubt show, appearances, order, dignity, cause a great deal of trouble. Very few would encounter them for the mere pleasure they give; nobody who is not thoroughly trained can maintain a consistent liking for them for their own sake; and men constantly sink into hugger-mugger from the mere weakness of their nature, and the infirmity of their resolution. They recognize in its dinginess something home-like and congenial with the humanity which arose from clay and will return to dust. Yet, of course, men are ashamed of this inclination in themselves. On no account must the world know it. Indeed, the world must have a wholly different notion of us, and be kept in the dark as to our little weakness; it must be ignorant of a hundred shifts which we positively relish putting ourselves to. Every position has its proper restraints, and no man has a right to profit by the privileges of a class and not conform himself to its obligations. All form, state, and order implies the interposition of some impediment to the immediate gratification of our natural wants, — the intervention, that is, of a medium, something that puts itself between the fingers and the dish; and the higher the station the more of these restraints intervene. We do not doubt that the poor find, without knowing it, a very material compensation for many of their privations in the prompt access they are permitted to such satisfactions as they have. Not but that the humblest cottage, decently ordered, abounds with checks. The cupboard and the stated meals constitute the discipline and order of myriads of households, and raise them above the hugger-mugger of others, where the loaf is always on the table, and not a moment is allowed to elapse between the sensation of hunger and its satisfaction.

Hugger-mugger, then, is the result of dislike, impatience, contempt, or mere slovenly neglect of the received class interpositions between our natural needs and their fulfilment. The mediums, no doubt, sometimes become excessive and irrational, and it is right to resist them; but the advocates for their disregard or suppression never treat them as restraints, and therefore as discipline, but only as ministering to the pride of man. Mediæval religion was in the habit of estimating a man's sanctity by the degree in which he dispensed with the restraints of the life to which he was born, and confined himself to the simplest wants, satisfied in the most direct and informal method. It was a point to keep the condition of the poor at its minimum of requirements; and what must many a hermit's cell have looked like and been, — rushes, maple-dish, and all, — if we once enter into the temptations to hugger-mugger of that sullen, solitary, negligent existence! It was in the same spirit that sour Presbyterians opposed every new refinement; and protested against the intervention of forks, with the argument that God gave men good meat, and they were become too proud to touch it with their fingers: whereas, in reality, to persons habituated to the simpler method, the new fashion must have been a considerable trial of patience: —

> "For much refinement, when it late arrives,
> May be the grace, not comfort of our lives."

And in this matter a school of philosophy has sided with asceticism. The new lights of the last century who advocated savage life were really exalting hugger-mugger. This was the teaching of "Sandford and Merton," impersonated in Harry, who contemned the order and state of Tommy's home, and for his part saw no use in any of those fine things, but only ate when he was hungry and drank when he was "dry." This was the meaning of that theory, so plausible to boyhood, that every man should be educated with a view to his being some day left to his own resources on a desert island.

If absolute equality were ever attainable, it must be through the means of hugger-mugger, which is the only true leveller; and it should be understood by every man who practises it, that he is doing his part to bring down his class to the one below it. It is sometimes quoted as an instance of noble simplicity that great people defy conventional regulations; but we maintain that when a duke carries his own carpet-bag, and a man of fortune travels second-class, or when anybody not pressed by absolute poverty allows himself to appear in sordid, ill-kept, slatternly attire, he is inflicting a blow on social order. What right has a man to enjoy all the distinctions and privileges of exalted station without its penalties? And to be waited upon, instead of doing things for himself, in spite of the honor of it, may be one of the most prominent of these penalties. In fact, to a man of an active, fussy temperament, being waited upon is often one of the greatest exercises of patience he can be put to. Indolence and practice combined, learn, indeed, to take it easily: the lady who summoned Quasha to tell Quaco to tell Fibba to pick up the pin that lay at her foot had to wait for her pin, and was resigned to the delay. But there are a hundred things that ought to be waited for rather than done irregularly by the principal's own hands, — an irregularity which it is a little penance to certain people to abstain from. Every nature has its own form of the temptation. There is the indolent and passive temper, that lets everything take its course, and sits in a muddle from mere weakness and poverty of spirit; and there is the restless and over-busy temper, that cannot endure to wait for the proprieties, and that reduces things to disorder and confusion from simple impatience of form and arrangement. To teach these busy people that things will be done though they do not do them is a rare triumph of training. Restless bodily activity which has once known the careless luxury of helping itself on every occasion, of dispensing with complications, is apt to become hopelessly unmanageable. There is a conceit in the doing things for themselves, a mistrust engendered by impatience, which makes these people the worst masters and mistresses in the world, and their houses the worst conducted; though the same temper would be invaluable in that condition where a man must do a thing himself or it will be undone, and where Nature's fine gentleman — serene in dignified confidence that the service will be rendered, and that, come what may, he shall never be subject to hurry, scuffle, and confusion — might be rather at a loss. This humble vice of doing what it is not our business to do is a subtle disqualifier for high place, if a man has ambition. This sham humility will keep him back, and tincture his manner with indecision and self-distrust, infused by the consciousness of being often in situations and positions which he would not choose the world to know.

Those men are powers in their own circle, and are secure of consideration and regard, who steadfastly resist hugger-mugger, and in their nature hate and abhor it, — who fight against it, never sink in their inner spirit beneath their own implied and avowed pretensions, are never caught at unawares, and are presentable down to every minute propriety. This state of things implies a habitual self-respect, a kind of sense of desert (not necessarily moral desert), and commands the deference which it tacitly claims. If a man shows, by his actions and his treatment of himself, his estimate of his own pretensions, others will acquiesce in it, — and with justice, for this is being true to one's self. Such a one is guided, not by what others see or think, but by an innate idea of fitness, a love of order and refinement for their own sake, whether other eyes are witnesses or not. But all this necessitates constant trouble and no end of sacrifices, and implies a very exceptional antagonism to all forms of muddle and incongruity; for habits of forethought, punctuality, precision, restraint, unremittingly practised in what seem small matters, involve greater self-control, and also greater strength of will, than far more conspicuous sacrifices made once in a way. Mr. Kinglake furnishes a pleasant example of this sort of hero in General Airey, who, when roughing it with his wife in a log-hut in West Canada, where his appointment lay, manfully resisted the all but irresistible blandishments of hugger-mugger: —

"Clad coarsely during the day, he was only to be distinguished from the other workmen by his greater activity and greater powers of endurance. Many English gentlemen have done the like of this, but commonly they have ended by becoming altogether just that which they seemed in their working hours, — by becoming, in short, mere husbandmen. It was not so with Airey. When his people came to speak to him in the evening, they always found him transformed. Partly by the subtle change which they were able to see in his manner, — partly, too, by so outward a thing as the rigorous change in his dress; but most of all, perhaps, by his natural ascendency, they were prevented from forgetting that their fellow-laborer of the morning was their master, — a master to whom they were growing every day more attached, but still their master."

The subtle change in manner was due, no doubt, to the associations of polished life connected with the ceremonious change of dress. Some people would have feared to seem finical, but "natural ascendency," in indulging its innate painstaking refinement, without which even ease is discomfort, had no such misgivings. On the other hand, there are persons whose plan and idea of life is absolutely opposed to this principle, — who would be hugger-mugger in a palace, from a positive taste for a shuffling sort of comfort, caring for nothing that does not tend to the lazy ease of the moment, and indifferent who knows and sees their ideal worked out.

From the time that Polonius was in "hugger-mugger" interred, —

> "No trophy sword nor hatchment o'er his bones,
> No noble rite nor formal ostentation," —

the word has never been used but with an implied apology, as if it were a rude term for a discreditable thing; and yet who shall say that there is not something endearing in it still? Perfect order is apt to be oppressive to poor human nature. We like one of these point-device people better, and feel vastly more at home with him, when we have found some flaw in his exactitude, some slovenly place about him. Let a large party be kept indoors through a long rainy morning, and by the end of it they will, if they are allowed to follow their instincts, be caught all collected together in the house's untidiest corner, — school-room, work-room, or lumber-room. The sight of disorder is a refreshing change, and unlocks heart and tongue. For health and spirits undoubtedly enjoy a momentary collision with confusion, perhaps because it imparts a sense of power to overcome it; while, on the contrary, invalids and melancholy persons have a natural horror of it even in its chance contact, as we see in their fastidious disgust for dust, disorder, and every form of bustling or shabby negligence.

In an occasional encounter with hugger-mugger undoubtedly lies one of the attractions of the annual seaside excursion. That liberty of dispensing with a hundred conventional necessities which belongs to lodgings in a crowded watering-place and to a sauntering out-of-door life — the feeling of roughing it, in careless defiance of home restraints — often imparts quite as keen an exhilaration, for a day or two at least, as the tumbling waves themselves. It is, for most people, the nearest practicable approach to that infantine dream of perfect felicity, — life in a travelling caravan, with feather-bed and blankets inside and a chimney at top. Many a reader has warmed to that scene of genial hugger-mugger in "David Copperfield," where the hero gives a dinner, and an almost raw leg of mutton offers an occasion for Mr. Micawber's talents in this line. He calls for a gridiron, and the formal company arrangements of the table are instantly broken up in a joyful confusion of hissing, spluttering chops, shirt-sleeves, and laughter. But Damocles's sword hangs over all these surreptitious joys, and it falls here most appropriately in the form of somebody's servant. It is, if we remember right, the villain of the story who keeps a butler, and this man enters when the fun is at its highest, and paralyzes the guilty assembly by the mere terror of his presence. And, in fact, servants are the great bugbears of all lovers of hugger-mugger for the mere comfort of it. If people anticipate their servants' duties, they are generally careful that the actual perpetrator of the forbidden toil should be anonymous. If a man carries his own portmanteau to his room, he would rather that the servant whose business it was to take it should not know how it came there. Servants, in fact, are quite right to despise any form of hugger-mugger, and to have pretty stringent ideas, too, as to what constitutes it, for this is necessary to their own sense of importance. If masters once helped themselves, their vocation would be gone, and the honors and credit of their profession extinguished. To be sure, a lazy fellow is willing that anybody should do his work for him, but he does not the less despise the doer as one who feels himself unworthy of his services; while he bestows all his willing attendance upon those who recognize his office and place, and accept the restraints, while they exact the privileges, of their own.

ATTENTION.

AFTER the first wants of nature are supplied, and amongst these we class not only material wants, but something to love and to care for, the one universal need is a certain amount of notice from our fellow-creatures, a home in the minds of others that we can take possession of at will, a ready, available interest in our ideas and opinions, — what we will here call Attention. Regard, respect, even affection, though they all infer a place in the minds of our friends, do not express the peculiar homage we would designate by this somewhat cold and formal word. We may be loved, honored, respected, and yet our admirers may take their own time to express their appreciation, and not attend to us when we are in the particular humor for their sympathy. All does not satisfy unless we have a hold, whenever we choose to assert it, over the mind and interest of others, — unless we can feel that then and there we have possession of them, — unless, in fact, we can command their attention, especially the attention of the choicest or most congenial minds within our reach. Truth is a fine thing where people can bear it, but there are truths which, in their naked austerity, human nature is not fit for; and the absolute amount of attention men gain when they are most anxious for it, and especially lay themselves out for it, is one of these. The work of a great many lives would stop if the workers realized how little their efforts are marked and regarded. The majority of men could not live happily if they did not live under a delusion in this respect. Of course, vain people are the greatest victims of the deception; but, in its degree, the craving for attention is as legitimate a longing as any other natural desire. Man, at his best, is so constituted as not to be able to separate himself from his work. He may, on the purest principles, desire the success of a great cause, but it costs an additional pang if not only the cause is slighted, but he himself is not attended to; while part of the charm of success is due, no doubt, to the sense of winning thought and sympathy in his own person. The vigorous, healthily constituted mind needs this essence of companionship, which is indeed the very sunshine of moral life. And yet we must all feel, if we reflect on our own habits of thought, that attention is a difficult effort, that it is a vastly more ambitious object of desire than to stand respectably with our neighbors, or to secure the substantial regard of our friends; that, in fact, we make a large demand upon others when we interrupt the current of their thoughts, and expect to divert them to our channel. Any favor that people can grant us is more under their own will than that prompt, earnest, exact attention which is the universal assumption on which all social intercourse is built; for we must act on the idea that attention is a much more attainable good than it can be proved to be. No doubt there are people who take for granted, in their own persons, that attention is no effort, as it never occurs to them to doubt that the amount of attention they receive from their friends is all right. But theirs is not of the quality most eagerly sought for. People instinctively look for an attention which costs something to the giver, which implies real labor, and a process of thought; only they don't always know that this is the real meaning of attention. However, this is the attention that men want, and it strikes us that very few people are philosophical enough and strong-minded enough to bear the knowledge of how little any effort can secure it as a habitual or permanent possession. For attention, with most of us, is such an unchainable thing — it is so essentially a man's own — that to pin it and fix it beyond the tampering of the owner is very much such an achievement as conjuring genii into a bottle. We mean such command over it as is implied by a man's voluntarily, for any unbroken length of time, suspending his own interests, speculations, or, more probably, vague reveries, and attaching himself to yours.

In the ordinary routine business of life it is scarcely a practical question. We must constantly act as though we were being attended to, whether we are or not. Indeed, we can scarcely be certain how matters stand, and must talk, express opinions, make speeches on the chance; but it will add greatly to our independence and serenity of mind if we realize something of the actual difficulty of bestowing the attention we profess to ask for, and the wondrous volatility of that faculty which we desire to hold suspended on our words. Our language has many golden forms of speech to tempt on ambitious or eloquent lips to feats of fine talking. We read of rapt, enslaved, charmed, fascinated, spell-bound attention, — of hearers hanging on men's lips, catching each accent as it falls, and the like; but every phrase really betrays that unassisted nature is not equal to the strain, and that magic art alone can master the universal rebellion. Again, we have plenty of terms expressive of the effort needed to secure this coy and fleeting good. The phrases, to awake, arouse, stimulate, attract, arrest attention, all testify to the toil and difficulty of the work; while the listener is not without an expressive vocabulary to convey the sufferings of forced, unwilling, jaded, weary, distracted, exhausted attention. He avenges himself on unworthy arts by a language of contempt for "claptrap," — for the dull spirits that reckon on a man's attention so long as they can forcibly "hold him by the button," — for those who use violence, and accomplish their end by "making folks stare."

The power of commanding the greatest possible share of attention, even by the most legitimate means, is perhaps not the sign of the highest intellect. Great intelligences can scarcely fail to shoot over the heads of commoner wits. A man must gain attention by assimilating himself to others, and adapting himself to their groove of thought. Thus Fenelon, who had this art to perfection, and charmed everybody that came near him, had a way of seeming to possess only just so much mind as the person he might happen to converse with, — he could talk exactly like an equal. And Sydney Smith, whose pen had the power of attracting universal attention to every cause he had at heart, did it by seizing just those points of a subject with which the majority felt most at home. This is not *commanding* attention, but engaging it by adapting yourself to the average tastes, perceptions, and opinions of mankind. A man is thus attended to by slipping into other people's ways of thought,—only investing their own ideas in a dress flattering to their self-love. In the same spirit, Mark Antony can afford to be modest; and humbly ask his countrymen to "lend him their ears," because he knows how to place his subject precisely on the level of their capacity. The matter that gains most ready attention in ordinary intercourse is easy, tolerably succinct, well-arranged narrative. We make no mention of wit or humor, because they are so short and flashing that they make no demand at all. The manner that secures it longest is a self-possessed, collected, determined one, unvisited by misgivings. When a man begins at the right end, and has a resolute clear grasp of his subject, he seems to have a claim on our attention; but all habits, tricks, and hesitations, as they betray failure of purpose, and weakness in his own hold, so they must detach and finally destroy ours. And yet how people will hum and ha,—their minds all astray, while they utter conventional or inarticulate sounds,—yet with unprincipled obstinacy refuse to release an attention which they have not vigor to keep in exercise! For, after all, attention is so far subject to the senses that, however profitless, imperfect, and irksome, it cannot be wholly suspended at will.

There can be no doubt that real attention is a great talent and a great power. Indeed, an extreme impatience of attention incapacitates a man for a place in the world. There is a morbid, demoralized state of mind in which men cannot listen. They cannot follow another man's train of thought, for they cannot give their mind into another's custody even for a moment. The very thought of it is an irritation and a bondage. This is a subject for compassion where men recognize their infirmity, and agree neither to give nor take; but we see it often in those who make large demands on the attention of others, and expect to be listened to at any length they choose. Again, there are people whose attention is simply criticism, — who are not capable of an instant's suspension of the judgment, — who accompany your words with a running commentary of protest or contradiction, showing that they have heard all, and attended to every word, but with none of the deference of a listener. But the mind needs unresisting, merely listening attention for its proper development; and this is one reason why the young ought to have the companionship of the young. Their elders are in such a relation to them that the mere act of silent attention might imply the sanction of a mature understanding, which of course the attention of equals does not; though impatient minds are too apt to suppose it does, and thus to lose substantial weight by mistimed interference. No man can be really influential who cannot listen as well as talk; and no one can know anything of the mind of others without attending in the simple, patient attitude of attention. He who can do this is, by the very gift, a comfort and stay to anxious, tried, and perplexed spirits, to whom the mere unfolding of their difficulties is often the best remedy. Experience seems to teach men endowed with conscientious attention that all people have something in them worth attending to. Their patience often helps them through a dull stratum into a vein missed by all others, but well worth working. Sir Walter Scott was one of these, and maintained that he learnt something from every one he travelled with. His biographer especially remarks on his serene attention to bores, and how graciously, through interminable prolixities, "the same bland eye watched the lips of the tormentor." To the bystander it was a mere exercise of courtesy and forbearance; but as no person can be charming without the appearance of attention, — and as in this case the appearance can scarcely exist without something of the reality, — the occasion was probably by no means so great an annoyance to the victim as to a circle assembled to hear Sir Walter Scott talk, not to listen to a discussion on the Truck System, or the Greek Epigram, as the case might be.

The mention of the bland eye brings us to the true test and sign of attention. Courtesy can control every other mark of roving thought, but no deception can be practised on the eye. If a man is not really attending, he cannot make his eye look as if he were. Either the iris is restless, or it is perceptible that its repose arises from thought turned inward; or, more hopeless still, the pupil is fixed in a determined, unmeaning stare. In any case, we have constantly to talk on. Things have to be said, and we must say them, and infuse into the so-called listener a general sense of our subject. But do not talk for the pleasure of talking, — for the mere relief of unburdening the mind to the wandering, the rigid, or the introspective glance. The owner of those eyes is wondering when you will have done, or he is absently occupied with his own affairs. Take the hint in good part, be as concise as you can, and relieve an unwilling, engaged attention. Now the bore is one who is not an observer of signs. He plods on, set on delivering himself of what he has to say, and so bewitched with the sound of his own voice that he does not mark, or, what is worse, is indifferent to, all evidences of fatigue or restlessness. No one need be a bore who notes the eyes and postures of those with whom he converses. No one need force himself habitually on the unwilling notice of others. On the other hand, there are eyes that invite confidence, — "bland," serene, clear-shining, out-looking eyes, at once patient and intelligent. This is the eye of the good listener. He keeps your pace; he goes with the fluctuations of fact or feeling or argument without effort. You may know you are not wearying him. Not that we would impose either upon a congenial glance or easy repose of attitude any unreasonable burden; but such people are not so common but that we should recognize them, and value them, when we see them. As it is, men constantly think they like and prize people for their talking, when it is in fact for their listening; and every kindly intelligent man who possesses this accomplishment is certain to win himself a great social reputation, and to be a pillar of any cause he takes up.

We have confined ourselves here to social attention, not the attention men give to books, or pay to young ladies, or bestow on their own business, or on works of benevolence. It is well that people should realize the difficulty of attention in its simplest form. If they do, they will not lay all the blame on their instructors if they find their attention restive and unmanageable under greater trials. That was a candid entry in Dr. Johnson's diary where he resolves "to attend the sermon unless attention be more troublesome than useful"; for at any rate it implied that attention was an effort. Most people assume that nothing is easier than to fix the thoughts on transcendent and often too unfamiliar ideas, and that, if their attention flags and wearies, of the two parties implicated in the transaction, it certainly is not themselves that are to blame.

Strong Wills.

IT is the fashion of our day to idolize the will. People good and bad, religious and profane, wise and frivolous, unite to honor persistent resolve. Strength of will is the staple of saints and sinners of any credit, magnitude, or popularity. It really matters very little with a great many people what the object may be, if it only be pursued perseveringly and remorselessly. Sin followed with a force to resist the blandishments of collateral sins becomes a virtue. Whenever a man has a great, prevailing, paramount desire which sets him above lesser, transient desires, be the main desire ever so truculent, mean, or base, he is the mark for some men's admiration and reverence, — not, indeed, in respect of the thing desired, but for the strength and persistence of his wish for it. The heroine of Mr. Wilkie Collins's "No Name" relies for our sympathy on this ground alone. If she were ever to swerve from her horrible and degrading purpose, if her resolve were to relax for a moment under the breath of any good or genial influence, the author would have no hope for her. He expects the public to like her because she stops at nothing to work her will. There is something in it, of course. There is a sort of virtue in being able to care for the same thing for a long time together. It is also a wonderful element of power. Lady Macbeth and Jezebel are more striking personages by far than their respective lords, — we might almost say that there is more to admire in them, — and this can be due to nothing else than their stronger wills. Nevertheless, all this talk about strong wills has something slavish and craven in it. It is a transfer of the allegiance from reason and right to brute force. It is the choice of control, of mastery by a strong hand, as owning our nature, not capable of free, intelligent action. Strength of will, in whatever cause, is pretty certain to surround itself with more or less of suffering, — not only its own voluntary suffering, but incidentally that of others. Like every other victory, it has its victims. A man unflinchingly working towards his aim may make a fine historical picture if he is engaged in a great cause, but a vast many wills go towards the grand display. Multitudes have to abandon their inherent rights in order to work out his purposes for him : and, therefore, to stand in open-mouthed admiration of mere strength of purpose, as such, is an act of subservience and a confession of weakness.

Not that the sentiment is always real. We admire strong wills most at a distance, when time or space separates us from their social consequences. As an active interference with our liberty, we are apt to see in it more of the unreasoning, and as we have said, brute element, than the divine. The strong wills we come in contact with have, unfortunately, more objects than one. A man in a book has a great revenge to arrive at through every obstacle, a great work to do in spite of all the world; and his will concentrates itself on the one object, and lets minor matters take their own course. But where it is a living propensity, it is prone to interference of the most annoying and ubiquitous kind, and is in no respect like the arrow flying at its mark, and touching nothing between. In fact, it is not at all a sublime thing to have a will stronger than our own wielded by an intelligence which, we flatter ourselves, is not in any respect above our own, controlling us, tampering with our liberty of action, and fumbling amongst all our prepossessions, — to feel ourselves thwarted at every turn by some influence which finds its happiness in arranging our affairs for us, and which somehow always gets its way. There are unquestionably minds of very small calibre, who do not thoroughly enjoy life unless they are habitually making the people about them do something they would rather not do, whose main pleasure in every scheme is to carry their point against the majority. We call this love of management; but what is it really but a busy, unsympathizing, narrow, often well-meaning mind under the spur of a strong will, working in some small, domestic sphere as many rulers and potentates have done in their great sphere who have gained immortal honor by permeating every nook and cranny of their dominions with their own individual sovereign will?

Seeing the inconveniences of this masterful impulse in the contracted range of each man's experience, we do not think that the will would have been lifted so high amongst the virtues by the unprompted homage of ordinary minds. People who make a business of thinking are at the bottom of it. It is they who have given form to what in others is but a vague yearning for the fixed, the definite, the irreversible. No doubt it is common to mankind to respect strength of any kind. It is not only women who want something stronger than themselves to lean upon. We are most of us tried by indecision. We are conscious of conflicting wishes, views, interests. We are harassed by doubt. We see two sides to most things, and are apt to be swayed by them alternately. Something perpetually steps in between us and our aim. We with difficulty hold on to our plans and schemes. Obstacles tell upon us; we accept omens, submit to hinderances. We give in and give up, we are hampered by self-mistrust, we balance the fors and againsts, we are subject to suspense of purpose and feeble volition. Freedom from doubt, consistency of intention, — these are something comfortable to rely upon. A man has weight with us who knows what he wants, and goes the straight way to get it, unvisited by our scruples and vacillations; though often this singleness of aim is due to certain intellectual deficiencies, and we should perhaps be amazed could we see the meagre, insufficient grounds for irrevocable decisions which a man would sooner yield his life than reverse. But it is with authors and thinkers by profession that this instinct of reliance grows into deliberate, willing subservience. Men forever engaged upon their own consciousness, — who turn every subject that comes before them inside out, — who balance, and weigh, and consider, and question, till certainty and choice seem to evade them, — are lost in admiration of a strong will displayed in triumphant, unscrupulous, overbearing action. They either do not know that the thing is done by not thinking, or they reverence it the more as intuition. They invest the phenomenon with a halo of comment as Germans do the text of Shakespeare; they enhance the rigidity of purpose, they give meaning to every accident. Obstinacy in error is sublime, stolidity is godlike. If these people only write like geniuses and live like other men, their respect for strength of will is rather abstract than practical; but there are keen, restless spirits who carry their speculative turn into private life and regulate their conduct by it. There are people who do everything by a conscious effort of thought, and theorize on every action as they perform it, — a practice wholly incompatible with a single aim, great or small. In its grand, sustained sense, versatile intellects cannot possess a strong will. Wilful enough they are, determined enough in their own way, but the way changes with every mood of thought. They see the merits by turn of every line of action, — are this day with the Epicureans, and the next with the Stoics; or for a change, one of these experimentalists decides to discard philosophy altogether, to do exactly like other people, to be minutely commonplace, not to take a step which has not the sanction of universal suffrage. A person thus proclaiming that he has no will of his own, and doing like other people with all his might, is a curious enough spectacle. He studies every motion, not crediting that anything can be done without design, — taking, as it were, every breath on reflection, and swallowing at well-considered intervals. With this state of things reason has little chance, for our friend can reason to a hair, and sees the weak side of every argument but his own. A coöl, steady will, having just what they want, and wanting all that they have, is the influence to manage these over-intellectual spirits. Anybody quite confident of his own line, and keeping to it, contemptuous of opposition, serenely and stolidly certain, is accepted as a guide by men worn out by too wide an embrace of every question. Only he must not be too clever, and he must never give reasons. Those they can dispute, but certainty and will are the things that they bow to as powers mysterious and divine. It is like the fable of the speculative young bear applying itself to the science of walking. "Shall I," says he, "move my right front paw first or my left, or the two front paws first or the two hind ones, or all four at once, and how?" fluctuating in all the endless alternatives which four legs offer, till will and action, in the person of the old she-bear, stept in to cut the knot, — "Leave off thinking and walk."

Will, then, as a power which attains its ends by a short cut, — which does while others think, and makes the world go its way, while intellect argues, refines, and beats about the bush, — is an object of genuine awe and reverence to metaphysical and speculative minds; but also it is made use of by a certain class of theorists (amongst the infinite number of subjects so applied) to talk nonsense about, and very deliberate nonsense we might suspect, but that fluent tongues can talk themselves into a partial belief of anything. Lecturers, either amateur or professional, are very fond of exalting the will. It is flattering to the vanity of an audience to be told that it only depends on themselves to be as powerful and successful as the great leaders of thought and action; and many speakers say it under the vague notion that, though it is not strictly true, it is a good, proper, stimulating thing to say. They know that the members of a Mechanics' Institute do not care to be taught out of the Catechism, yet the occasion enjoins a moral, and utility is the order of the day. Especially if they themselves are at the top of the tree, it looks and feels like humility to assure every raw youth of the company that he has only to try, with a will, and he may attain to the speaker's level. Only set your hearts, he cries, — in spite of a conviction deep inside, giving the lie to his words, — only resolve, with an intense, continuous act of volition to do and to be such-and-such things, and you will infallibly succeed. "How many men have begun as you have, and ended by being partners where they were errand-boys! How many have begun with twopence, — possibly the sum in your pockets at this moment, — and ended life the owner of half a million! How many have begun mere journeymen, as some of you are, and risen to be inventors, discoverers, the everlasting benefactors of mankind! And any of you may do the same if only you have a will strong enough. All these men had a will; they never gave in; they suffered no pleasure to allure them from the one object of their lives; they conquered all difficulties; they were proof against disappointment; hence your Fairbairns, your Stevensons, and all the merchant princes of the land." Facetious allusions are possibly thrown in to Whittington and his master's daughter, or that beggar-boy of Florence, who, receiving an alms from a fair maid of high degree, incontinently resolved to make her his wife, left the city on the instant a soldier, and came back generalissimo, to claim and win his reward. Fortunately for the audience, these ideas never enter the mind beyond infusing a temporary unmeaning inflation. The errand-boy cannot get up the sublime preliminary will which is to set the rest in motion. A will, unprompted by power to work it out, is nothing. Nor will conceit of power do much. A few rebuffs and failures abate pretension, except where vanity impairs the sanity of the brain. If people did not know all the while that men cannot make fortunes in business without a good head for it, and that it is no use being persevering over mechanics unless you have more than average of the gifts for the work, — if they did not know hundreds of plodding, indefatigable clerks, who yet remain clerks all their lives, — this theory of the will would make lunatics of a docile audience.

Yet, though all the harm which might follow, if such advice were capable of being acted upon, does not come, yet some harm always results from the wide diffusion of untruth, and the continual utterance of swelling words, even if everybody knows that they mean nothing. Not but that there is a will that makes a man; but it cannot be put into him, and, indeed, needs no prompting. A man starts on his career with a tacit understanding with himself that he is to rise. It is a step-by-step progress. He probably has no distinct aim. It is only in books that he resolves from the first dawning of ambition to become owner of such an estate or bishop of such a see. But he means to get on, and devotes all his powers to that end. He fixes his thoughts beyond immediate self-indulgence, chooses his friends as they will help the main design, falls in love on the same principle, and, habitually deferring to a vague but glowing future, learns to work towards it, and for its sake to be self-denying and long-sighted. His instincts quicken; he puts forth feelers, which men who take their pleasure from hand to mouth have no use for; he lives in habitual caution, with an eye always awake to the main chance. Thus he refines and enhances that natural discretion which doubles the weight and value of every other gift, and yet keeps them on an unobtrusive level — leaving itself the most notable quality — till he is universally pronounced the man made to get on, by people who do not know that it is a steady will that has made him and kept him what he is.

This is the will strong for itself. It, in fact, pushes others aside, takes their places, holds on its fatal course; but, as being unobtrusive and never openly asserted, it is the direct opposite of the meddlesome will of our social experience, expressed in the phrase that such a person must always have his way. Both are varieties from the historical or romantic will, which makes great heroes, criminals, tyrants, or martyrs, according to the cause in which it is applied. We believe, even on this grand heroic scale, many a will gets worshipped in manhood which acts precisely on the same motive for which an obstinate child gets whipped, — that is, the man goes on because he has begun. Nevertheless, we all feel a vigorous will to be a fine thing. It is a stroke of nature in the man in the play to hate a bird that does not know its own mind. It is wearisome to be with people without any will of their own. Volition is life; no one can be really great, whatever his other powers, without it; nor can a man cultivate it in himself too carefully, so long as he respects the free will of others, and only applies it to secure constancy in purposes and decision in action.

TALKING OF SELF.

IT is a nice and a curious inquiry how far it is desirable, or even tolerable, for people to talk of themselves. There is no broader distinction between man and man than the manner and the degree in which this is done. There are people who never talk of themselves. There are others who never talk of anything but themselves, — that is, who can pursue no subject unless the vista can be made to terminate in self. Wherever it comes to this, the question admits but of one answer, — indeed, society has put the too frequent use of the word "I" under an interdict. No person who mixes much with mankind dares to turn the conversation habitually upon himself, except under some feint or disguise. Nevertheless, we all of us know persons who talk only of themselves, and families who never get farther from themselves than one another. These are probably the dullest people and dullest families of our acquaintance; for, when we come to think of it, all prominent dulness has a touch of egotism at bottom, and this is the point that tells. It is the part we have to play in their company that oppresses us both at the time and in recollection. Not only is their intelligence chained to themselves, but ours also. All interchange and variety of thought are impossible, not only because they are a heavy, unimaginative sort of people, whose flights are circumscribed to their own prospects, but because their one subject is precisely that on which we can neither speak our own mind nor satisfy expectation. We could discuss the man merrily enough behind his back; but to be forced to follow his lead, too polite to be candid, yet full of inward revolt, is a false position, and the inevitable subservience leaves a flavor of annoyance and failure which intercourse with mere dryness and insipidity cannot be charged with.

We all know men and women tethered, by a string whose length we instinctively measure, to themselves. Every subject under the sun reminds such people of themselves. Nothing is too remote for this alliance, — they cannot hear of the stars without wanting their own horoscopes. Their sole notion of conversation is to display themselves. They are ready to unveil their whole idiosyncrasy to whoever will look and listen. Their loves and hates and prospects are at anybody's service. Their experiences, successes, every fine thing ever said to them or of them, are common property. The whole world is their confessor in the matter of their faults, temptations, whims, grievances, doubts, and weaknesses. They expect to interest strangers by an avowal of their taste in meats and drinks and clothes. They confide their diseases and their remedies, their personal habits, their affairs to any chance comer, never for a moment visited by the misgiving pressed upon them by the preacher,— "Is it possible that it should never come into people's thoughts to suspect whether or not it be to their advantage to show so very much of themselves?" Society, or rather their own little world, is simply a tablet on which to subscribe self. When forced by some strong counter-will out of this indulgence, they are visibly at sea, vacant, disturbed; they have nothing to say: we feel for them as painfully out of their element, and are prone, in weak good-nature, to help them into port again. Now, a good deal of this is mere ill-manners. People who talk in this way are either underbred or incapable of nurture, or they suffer the want of certain wholesome restraints that keep the rest of the world in order. Miss Austen, whom few forms of social folly escaped, has more than one character representing this habit of mind, and revealing its source. Every reader can recall that elaborate and inimitable impersonation of self-display, Mrs. Elton, who, once received into the memory, has too many counterparts in real life ever to be forgotten.

Vanity is of course the leading motive to this obtrusive display. Yet the habit of perpetually reverting to self is not always to be confounded with vanity. Mere paucity of ideas and deadness of fancy drive some people into it who have a willingness to talk, and yet so little perception of things out of themselves that nothing apart from their own routine of sensations presents itself to say. No doubt it gives them a general sense of importance to clothe themselves in words, but they have hardly a choice as to the means. There are men who will tell anybody how often they have been jilted, under the vague sense that honor will somehow redound to themselves from the confession; or they will found a claim for distinction upon weak digestion, or the difficulties they encounter in shaving. But these aspirations are something apart from vanity. There is a mild satisfaction in being not a mere insignificant unit, but possessed of differences and peculiarities, which is worth all the world besides to some people, and indeed to which none of us are quite insensible. Others talk of themselves from a nervous desire to cover their defects, — a restless impulse to set off their presentable points. They are alive to some weak side, which preys on their sensitiveness: as the people most apt to talk of their fine friends and grand relations are those who are deeply conscious of a preponderance of the other sort. Thus very few persons who talk much about themselves talk the truth. The impression they want to give is one-sided. There are probably a hundred things about themselves which, in the midst of ostentatious candor, they suppress.

> "Some faults we own; but can you guess?
> Why, virtues carried to excess."

And the side represented swells to inordinate dimensions, and takes an aspect bearing it out of the region of fact. Or perhaps, like Goethe and Rousseau, they have a notion that everything becomes them, — that even meanness or baseness is glorified when made a matter of frank confession.

As excessive talk of this kind is presumption, the habit is most odious in young people. Children in their natural state never talk of themselves. They show egotism by a peculiar appreciation of the pronouns "my" and "mine"; but they are not yet self-conscious. They could not, if they would, unveil themselves, — their vanity takes another direction. All attempts, unless very systematic and insidious, fail to rouse self into expression. Precocious children now and then talk of themselves, especially if forced and excited by a certain sort of religious teaching. Then they can be heard to enlarge with a horrible glibness on their feelings, their convictions of sin, their schemes for setting the world to rights; but this is mostly a sign of an overtasked brain, accompanied sometimes by an exceptional, grotesque form of naughtiness, and sure to pass off as the health improves and the cleverness vanishes. When childhood, and even boyhood, is fairly over, is the time for self to assert itself in talk. Then it awakes full armed in a sort of bloom and overflow of conceit, an invasion of arrogance never to be matched in after life. There are not many more unpleasant things in the social world than a pert, forward young man, whose theme is universally himself, — who entertains every company with himself, and breaks up every conversation that does not concern himself. These insufferable persons are of all sorts, from the flippant and most bearable who clamors of his own exploits, boasts himself the envy of one sex and the idol of the other, to the deep, oracular, and enlightened youth who will not allow us to remain in the dark as to his views on any of the topics that occupy mankind. Or there is the sententious, didactic young man, more than endured probably by some small admiring circle, — a teetotaler, perhaps, or a stringent Sabbatarian, or engaged in a course of lectures to "the lower orders," or in some way or other a conscious example, reprover, and guide to his fellow-men. Whatever their line, they are intrinsically the same, — all alike patronizing or indifferent to their betters, — all blind to the impression they make, — all lavishing the fulness of their admiration, reverence, and talk on one central figure, — all flaunting the same self in our eyes, — keeping up the one chorus, "I, I, I," "I say," "I know," "I do."

And yet all people must sometimes talk of themselves, — all ought to be able to do it on fitting occasions freely and naturally. No man is interesting who never talks of strictly personal matters; indeed, we cannot be said really to know anybody till he has talked of himself to us. Until there has been a mutual interchange of such confidences, people are acquaintances, not friends; and the man who has no such confidences to make has no friends. It is not, then, the practice itself, but how and when to indulge it, that is the point. We use the word "indulge" designedly, for unquestionably the subject most interesting to every one must be himself. It is in recognition of this fact that all popular forms of religion agree in spiritualizing egotism. Methodism enjoins all its members to enlarge periodically each on himself, — the only check being that all have to listen in their turn. Romanism makes asceticism endurable by enjoining an immense amount of self-scrutiny and proportionate self-portraiture; and attempts at conventual life in our own Church all bring out the fact that unlimited dwelling on self and lengthy confession — that is, the talking of self — is the one indemnity for a life of unnatural constraint and bondage. To persons open to the active interests of life and the relaxations of society, however, a great many circumstances ought to combine to make the subject of self a natural or even a pleasurable one. Talking of self is one of the strongest proofs of confidence that can be given by a mind of due delicacy and reserve, — a confidence that ought to be bestowed with such discretion as to make it always welcome. With ordinary people, under ordinary circumstances, the subject, at any length or particularity, must be either a favor or an impertinence. There are, however, a great many people who have a right to talk of themselves with freer latitude than it is wise to give ourselves, — old people, for instance, who have the instinctive longing to leave some record of themselves behind them. Even where old age "is given to lying" of past achievements, it is not so bad as the boasting of younger men. There is generally some quaint savor about it, — some illusion of a failing memory claiming our indulgence in the worst cases, and softening contempt. Invalids and persons of weak nerves and spirits must be allowed to talk of themselves. Pain, weariness, and seclusion throw them upon their inner consciousness. When every nerve and function of the body makes itself felt, and every feeling is morbidly excited, they must be excused if nothing out of themselves can command their attention. It is needless to say that persons under some immediate shock, unhinging to the whole being, must be not only allowed, but encouraged to talk of themselves; for a personal grief put into words is infinitely lighter and more bearable than trouble pressing on the heart. There is something in every effort at expression which brings relief; and when sorrow can be brought to describe itself, the worst is over. Again, persons of notoriety may be pardoned if they fall into this habit. We hear of great poets, authors, preachers, philanthropists, soldiers, who talk too much of themselves; and it is true that vanity is often a conspicuous element in conspicuous greatness, acting as a sort of spur, and indemnifying itself with words. But society itself takes the part of flatterer in their case, — first leads them on, and puts them off their guard by the importunity of its interest, and then of course betrays them.

And lastly, wits make great capital of themselves. Many of the best things of our most delightful humorists are about themselves. We not only excuse it in their case, but this perpetual consciousness of and reference to themselves is of the essence of their wit, and gives it its careless, genial character. So far from any sense of restraint when Falstaff or Sydney Smith talk of themselves, it has the effect of making us all partners in the joke. But in every case where it is so, it is not the man's real self, but one or more of his personal or mental characteristics, that he plays with. We are conscious all the while of an inner self, which he keeps as jealously guarded as the most reserved of his hearers. That talk of self, or any part of self, which connects the speaker with grotesque, remote, abstract, or strongly-contrasted ideas, is more than tolerable. That which keeps down both speaker and listener, in whatever seeming variety of subject, to one tedious, obtrusive idea, is the propensity under which society rebels. After all, it is a matter of sympathy. The sinners in this line have no fellow-feeling. They do not do as they would be done by, for they see no parallel between themselves and others, their own affairs and other people's. They believe in a distinct superiority in all that concerns themselves. Trifles in the abstract are not trifles with them, but subjects of legitimate interest to the world; and that obtuseness which constitutes want of sympathy is at the bottom of their error. Any person who can make his inner self or his family affairs amusing has perception enough to secure his hearer's interest before he tries it. Indeed, a man may say and do anything, — he may enumerate his charities, he may detail his last quarrel with his wife, he may repeat a string of his own *bon mots*, or press upon strangers the perusal of his manuscript poem, — he may offend against every principle and every canon of taste; but so long as he excites a genuine interest, and relies on real sympathy, he is not the man we mean, and does not offend in the particular direction which has given rise to our strictures.

FOLLY.

WISE men and keen-witted men have so long occupied themselves with the nature of folly and the analysis of fools, that the subject might seem to be exhausted; but it is a feature of folly, that nothing can be understood about it without personal experience. We know a fool when we see him, but not before. Nothing that other people tell us exactly tallies with this knowledge. Sprightly, energizing folly takes us by surprise as long as we live; we never get so used to it as to know what is coming. Thus the folly of mankind supplies it with its surprises; it is a stimulant to curiosity never allowed to slumber. The dullest neighborhood, — the freest from rational excitements, — is enlivened at intervals by the scintillations of some fantastic folly or another. It is not too much to say, that half the lively *con amore* talk of social life owes its briskness to this source; nor does this necessarily imply preference for the subject, for it is of the essence of a fool to be always thrusting himself on people's notice, to be doing something to be talked about.

"Ma'am," said one of the sisterhood of Mrs. Gamp to a client, "you can never be too thankful that your children be n't born fools." Let us at once explain that, if they had been, they would not have supplied us with an illustration. It is said by one of our essayists, in contrasting folly with affectation, that nature may sometimes make a fool, but never a coxcomb. But we are not willing to believe that the folly that plays so great a part in the world is a taint in the blood. The fools we mean are not simply dull, — on the contrary, they are clever fellows. "An eminent fool must be a fool of parts." To figure in this department needs great self-reliance, and even powers of invention. Simple weakness of intellect, mere incapacity, can never make itself conspicuous. Some sharpness is necessary for every sort of prominence. Folly is not folly till it proclaims itself. When Cymon

> "Durst not begin
> To speak, but wisely kept the fool within,"

he was ceasing to be a fool. What, indeed, we might ask, do the wisest do more? It is vigorous, acting, self-confident folly that gets talked about. Minds of this mould are of the sanguine temperament, and find a sprightly joy in self-display of any kind. If they are but making themselves seen, they believe they are doing well for themselves; and even where they blunder and flounder, they do so under the complacent conviction of a triumph. They are never ashamed. They prefer their folly to anything else about themselves, and boast of any action especially silly all their lives. It is this particular feature which separates essential folly from what may be called accidental, contagious, or sympathetic folly, — the effect of blinding or absorbing passion which takes a man out of himself, as anger, ambition, jealousy, revenge; or of some popular hallucination possessing multitudes at the same time, as table-turning, collecting of old postage-stamps, frenzy for sights not worth seeing, and the like. Folly has been pronounced, on the highest authority, a necessary condition of one passion to which commonplace mortals are far more prone than fools: —

> "For to be wise and love
> Exceeds man's thoughts, — that dwells with gods above."

It is too universal an experience, that lovers in the climax of their felicity are foolish, to prove anything against the individual; it is rather a "sweet, wise madness," towards which the most churlish are indulgent, as testifying to the genuineness of the fortunate distemper. But the perpetrator of occasional follies is not so indulgent towards himself. He cannot always forgive himself excesses that his friends look over; and, from whatever source, the greater follies of his life plant a sting in the memory.

Folly, to be folly proper, is an abiding flaw or leakage, of which we are made continually aware. Yet the tendency to folly constantly looks like cleverness in children, and may be fostered as such. The wise child has the same thoughts as the foolish child, but recognizes them as foolish or impertinent, and suppresses them; while the other, impelled by the craving for self-exhibition, which is an essential ingredient of folly, thinks alone of notice and attention. A sensitive mind very early occupies itself with what passes, or is likely to pass, in the mind of others, — a great check to display; but, perhaps, if we must name one unfailing characteristic of a fool, it is the want of power to see himself and his doings reflected in the mind of other men. To know with absolute correctness how we stand in the thoughts of others is given to none; but in the case of the foolish person there is an utter gulf between his idea of himself and the consent of mankind concerning him. Again, it is a sort of crowning victory of reason and good sense to realize how small a space for good or ill we occupy in men's thoughts at any given time.

This knowledge would be intolerable to the man void of understanding. Thus he will always be talking, and always in a bustle. He is restless if not doing, — and doing, not for the thing's sake, but for other people to see, satisfied if he can only make them stare. The fool proper is always more foolish inside than out. He can never be said to reflect, or to perform any processes of mental digestion. He is always standing in his own light. Thus he reads without getting at the drift, hears without attending, laughs without point, acts without realizing consequences, is confident without grounds, is blind to impossibilities, does not see the connection of cause and effect, lives without gaining experience, never recognizes a heart, reality, or meaning in anything, and knows nothing of all this, and is perfectly satisfied with himself through it all. And this from no want of natural perception, but from contempt of the safeguards without which the wisest fall into the same errors, — from the habit of viewing things, not for themselves, but solely as they suggest opportunity of display, and can be twisted into an occasion for thrusting Self forward. A great deal of the folly of the world consists in people thinking themselves wiser than all the rest of mankind, because they are too curiously possessed and preoccupied by themselves to entertain the claims of others, or to conceive of merit outside their personal consciousness. There are people who do not see why they should ever be mere learners, — who affect to make discoveries in a science of which they know nothing, and will strike out new views on subjects to which they have not devoted an hour's reflection, and which the smallest reach of thought beyond the walls of their brain would show them to be the lifelong occupation of superior, trained, experienced minds. Foolish people of this class think their own hap-hazard worth more than the tact of an expert or the conclusions of patient labor, because they know nothing of the workings of other minds, and therefore have no respect or reverence. The fool is conceited more from blindness to the merit of others, from recognizing no superiority, than from any deep-seated pride in his own acquirements.

All these are irritating enough characteristics. To have to act with a fool is to involve one's self in confusion and contempt. Nothing is more wearing than intimate intercourse with folly, — nothing more intolerable, we should suppose, than to be under the dominion of fools. It shrivels up heart and brain. To live with a person who sees nothing by the clear light of reason, who never reaches the cause and motive of things, who is always mistaking sham for reality, who perverts everything into a fantastic occasion of display, and involves all about him in the ridicule of his proceedings, sours the temper and embitters life. It has, then, to be accounted for why the subject of folly and the delineation of fools should be such a perennial source of amusement to mankind, — why what crushes the spirit forced into too close connection with it should be so diverting to hear of; why a course of action which afflicts its victims with a dreary sense of monotony and hopeless repetition should present such a startling succession of new effects at second hand. That the subject has a very remarkable fascination we just now cannot doubt. One of our theatres has lately devoted itself for a year and a half to the impersonation of a fool, and the world showed no weariness or satiety. Lord Dundreary would be dreadful in actual companionship; but under Mr. Sothern's management people found him excellent sport, and enjoyed his inanities over and over again. This may be thought a sign of a frivolous taste in a vitiated public; yet how is it that our wittiest satirists, our deepest and truest observers, our profoundest moralists, have been alike attracted, and have expended their best efforts on this subject, not only in portraying the folly of mankind, but in singling out individual instances from real life, or creating them with a sort of inspired truth of imagination? Indeed, as "true no-meaning puzzles more than wit," it calls for the exercise of the highest powers to portray a fool to the life. Good common-sense can often give a fair picture of a wise man; but to follow the mazes of a perfectly frivolous and unreasonable mind, — to distinguish the nice varieties of folly, — to keep distinct each separate vein, — to show how self reigns in all, under such infinite diversities of vanity, pomposity, affectation, and whim, demands real genius and the courage of intuitive perception. Moreover, many characters depicted by the highest genius are painful to the reader; we give a sort of unwilling tribute to the skill and power of the delineation, but a well-drawn fool wins cheerful appreciation, — he is a joy forever. Writer and reader are sure to be of one accord.

This general delight in the safe and distant contemplation of folly will perhaps be attributed to pride, — to a sense of gratified superiority. There are people with whom pride is a universal solution, and in this case with some appearance of reason. If the picture is well-drawn, we are sure to know or to have known some man or woman very like it; and there is all the satisfaction of a hit. It is undoubtedly pleasant to be let into these little confidences by the more penetrating minds; our own capacity brightens under the stimulus. A man never in his own person feels so little like a fool as when some masterpiece of this school is put before him. But we must think that the attraction of folly lies mainly in its being so intensely human, and at the same time divested of the awe and mystery attaching to all that is unfathomable and beyond us in the higher characteristics of our nature. There is so much in the grander forms of humanity that takes us beyond our knowledge; we get so soon into the dark, and have to grope our way. All other creatures have some depths that are not fathomable,—something that reaches beyond the visible into dimness and the terrors of the unseen, something which inspires the timidity of conscious ignorance; but the fool is essentially superficial. People who are not fools are superficial too; but they recognize something in others to which they defer, though they cannot sympathize with it, and on which they act and plan. But folly is so all outside,—it has so little perception of what is not expressed by signs and acting, that there is not even reflected depth or mystery. There is no shade about it; it stands in the bare light of common day, removed at the farthest point from our superstitions, hedged about by the comfortable security of every-day human nature. However eccentric its manifestations, it acts on some principle or design easy to understand. We can only mistake in the interpretation of it by probing for a meaning; for folly pure and abstract is all surface, and incapable of seeing or apprehending anything beyond the senses.

It is this singleness of view which imparts to the entirely superficial their readiness on every social demand for feeling. They are up in the appropriate signs, which they quite believe are all that the thing itself signifies. When Silence moralizes on death, Shallow is prompt with the right thing to say:— "Certain, 't is certain, very sure, very sure; death, as the Psalmist saith, is certain to all; all shall die. How a good yoke of bullocks at Stamford fair." What more can friendship or the thought of death demand of us? Folly is always more than ready for all the solemn occasions of life, only it welcomes each harrowing or trying event of existence as a sort of game of skill. There is something to be done to show that the position is understood, and the only way that occurs of proving this is by overdoing the signs. Hence the broadest of black borders and emulation in funeral trappings, under the notion that grief must be there if there be only crape enough to swathe it in. Hence, solemn seclusions and a perfect get-up of despair, till the whole is cast off at a moment's warning, and some new effect struck out, without any consciousness that there has been a performance, or that real sorrow is a wound, an aching want of something lost and never to be restored. It is the same with all the sentiments and affections. Folly delights in, dotes on them all, and expatiates in romance, benevolence, friendship, enthusiasm, even remorse; only it does not know what any of them mean, beyond certain shows and exhilarating opportunities for doing something, outvying others, and making an appearance. It has no idea of any out-of-sight emotion. It is the busy, pretentious assumption of these qualities, and the break-down, the bathos, from the absence of the essence of them, — from the want of an inner prompter, — it is the eagerness to be well with the world, and the fantastic expedients for effecting its desires, it is the grotesque and yet the servile imitation of feeling, thought, and sense, which produces the succession of bizarre effects so delightful to gossip. A foolish person is always doing something silly and to be talked about; he has no other world than other men's eyes and tongues; if only plenty of these are occupied with him, his ideal is fulfilled, and the world is quite ready to make it a bargain.

We cannot imagine mere inconsequence, conceit, and folly having any part in another existence. As we have said, it is essentially human. It is not an impulse or instinct, or any secret inner influence; it is the flutter of superficial humanity, bounded by the senses: it belongs to our present ignorance, weakness, and blindness. So soon as we are actuated by a deep motive, we are no longer foolish. By whatever means the veil is lifted up, we are among realities. We want no other argument than this to prove that the spiritualistic communications from another world are an imposition. Their utterances are foolish, the clumsy expedients of thumps and raps and riotous furniture are foolish, and, if foolish, nothing can persuade us but that flesh and blood have a hand in them.

Many a reader will perhaps feel that we have not even touched the sort of folly he is best acquainted with. Every one old enough to observe knows some signal, as it would seem some exceptional, example of folly. Every class of men, every walk of life, however high and solemn its intellectual pretensions and requirements, has, in presence or memory, some particular and eminent fool connected with it. As Johnson says of Shakespeare, making free with Roman greatness, "He wanted a buffoon, and went to the Senate-House for what the Senate-House was sure to supply." There have always been, and always will be, foolish justices, foolish judges, foolish members of Parliament, foolish speech-makers, foolish preachers, foolish authors, foolish celebrities of all kinds; and these not the least considered of their class, for there is this in lively and energetic folly, with its serene self-consequence and insensibility to snubs, its courage and obtrusive vigor, — qualities which have the gift of making their way and keeping uppermost, — it does somehow fit into the existing state of things. Those who fail in life's struggles are not the fools, or, at least, not what are called such. There are people besides King Charles who never say a foolish thing, but who, if things went by their right names, and were tested by the end, are no doubt the greatest fools of all. But we have kept to that recognized acceptation of the term which has to do with the comedy of life, as the other has with its tragedy.

To conclude, it is not everybody that knows the difference between folly as a quality and doing foolish things, which the wisest do in their time. A clear-sighted observer is slow to impute that intrinsic, pervading folly which, in its excesses, marks and separates a man. Mere satirists like to class all mankind under this head, because men can be convicted of absurdities in concert, and because they are, one and all, occasionally foolish. The test is, Do they ever wake to a consciousness of having played the fool? No man who is ever thoroughly, deeply, heart and soul, ashamed of himself, — who comes to a sense of the true nature of his own folly, and sees it with other men's eyes, — should be classed among the irreclaimable. The real fool never regrets the right thing or for the right reason, and under no circumstances sees himself as others see him.

Time Past.

EVERY mode of viewing time is so trite, every turn of expression about it has become such a commonplace, that it is really one of the hardest things we know to think about time at all, — to bring the mind to face the idea. The preacher moralizes about time, and the historian marks out its course; we observe times and seasons, and keep birthdays, and have watches and clocks, and prose about the flight of time, and lay plans to get rid of it, and note its ravages on our friends, and have qualms at our first gray hair, and assume that we were born into time, and profess that we expect to die and have done with time altogether. But with all this array of testimony, the thought rarely comes home; the thing is apprehended but by glimpses and snatches, reaching us, when it does come, by a side-wind and at unawares. How can we realize time but through ourselves, — through our own part in it? To be sure, we are the heirs of all the ages; but everything works against a true sense of our inheritance, — against our connecting ourself with what went before our spark of life was set alight. The materialists will not believe in eternity, but, practically, this is easier to believe in than in a beginning and an end altogether distinct from our personality. Education, of course, strives to infuse this belief; but in spite of the labors of childhood to impress it, written history leaves but a faint stamp on many minds, — often none at all on the uneducated. It never quite passes for reality. Its facts do not feel like the facts with which we have to do. It is the difference between direct evidence and circumstantial. How many are aware of a sort of spring or clutch of the mind, as at a sudden revelation, — a change from shadow to substance, — when events and persons that are passing into the cold Valhalla of history reach us in some more vital way. Thus the old President of Magdalen had seen Dr. Johnson, and described the "brown tradesman's wig" with a memory that could still recall the uncouth figure. Here, then, was a man who had actually seen Johnson, who in his turn had seen Queen Anne. From a Stuart we seemed helped on somehow to a Tudor, from a Tudor to a Plantagenet; everything gained body and truth, from the share our senses had in the first start, — our hold on the first link. An *editio princeps*, an old letter with the post-mark, a portrait, a trustworthy relic, anything that brings us in fancy face to face with the original, gives an impression of genuineness otherwise unattainable, to a multitude of minds who know the facts to which it bears witness only by the common hackneyed way; and strengthens it in all. We pass from conventional belief to something more actual; we realize a space of time; we take a leap through intervening years and ages. Nor need the space be long, — it need only be well out of our own experience. The grasp of the past, no doubt, is overpowering, on bringing to light an Assyrian bull, or an Etruscan king lying in state, or a family group at Pompeii; but if we were so very sure about Ben Jonson, Dryden, and the rest, how came that thrill connecting us with those names when our youth first saw them in the Poet's Corner? For an instant, we knew that there was a world before we lived in it. Not that at any age we consciously question, much less dispute this fact, but we have a momentary sense of companionship with certain past existences, — of itself telling a tale as to our ordinary attitude of thought towards them, — which extends our tenure of time, while it constitutes, for the objects of this faith, the immortality they sighed for; such sighs proving that the imagination of poets gets a stronger hold of the idea of time than ordinary faculties can attain to. Nothing, however, can be more transient than these convictions. The experiment does not answer twice. Our belief soon starves on such food.

But time has less genial ways of proving its independence, by forcing on us an intolerable sense of isolation. Time is short, and life is short; but shorter than either is our share in the time and thought of others. When we are with the very young, it is often borne on us that large tracts of our life are, and must ever remain, utterly unconnected with them; that what is present to us — for all memory is a sort of present time — is history to them; that our boyhood, our youth, the events that absorbed us and determined our course, are to them matters of faith, like Alexander the Great or William III., — things with which they can have no personal concern, no connection but through an unimpassioned, indulgent sympathy. We feel that to them, all these are simply some of the myriads of things that happened before they were born; that they do not, cannot know *us*, but only just that slip and slice of ourselves that runs parallel with their existence; and again, that when we are gone, they must still have as warm an interest in the world, as busy a life, — that babes yet unborn will interest them, fill their thoughts, be their friends, marry them perhaps, while we shall be but a memory, a thing past by, inevitably dimming away towards indistinctness and forgetfulness. Of course, will be the reply; what can be more palpably, more grossly obvious? No doubt it is so; but still, there is a clash between feeling and dry knowledge; and there are a good many people with whom the feeling makes the more influential impression. How is it, one asks, while we are all to ourselves, our own universe, the centre of things, round which everything turns, and for which everything was created, through which alone we can realize existence, thought, life, matter, — how is it that all these servants and attendants upon us go on without us? The cynic who wrote, in scorn, of this yearning selfishness, —

> "The sun has rose and gone to bed,
> Just as if Partridge were not dead," —

yet shows a passing apprehension of the pang and the qualm which each man feels for himself at some moment or other, in rebellion against that dull forgetfulness which is some day to swallow him up. It is the same sensation which led Dante to ask, in solemn wonder, of the chance stranger arriving at his city, how he could have private cares that day that Beatrice had died? We believe there are persons to whom the notion of the world they know, apart from themselves in it, is so impossible, — who understand their own existence so much more keenly than anything else, — that practically they think the world will end with them. *Après moi le déluge*, represents not at all an uncommon posture of mind. It is a mere chance whether this temper leads such persons to talk of heaven under the notion that earth will not exist after they have left it, or to keep a hold on time, and "fix their memory with a thousand nails," by clogging posterity with plans and restrictions and the incubus of a dead will, as though their volition was to survive, a power and an influence controlling future generations. Anything is more natural and more possible than that things should go on without them.

But, apart from this madness of a strong will, all thoughtful minds would willingly take note of time, and keep what hold they can on past and future, —

> "And I could wish my days to be
> Bound each to each with natural piety."

What effects this, — what holds the individuality together under the shocks of perpetual change, — is association. There are certain landmarks of memory, connecting especial occasions and impressions with persons and localities, and so giving a point to periods of time, and constituting them stepping-stones over the inevitable lapse and flow of unregarded moments. He is only half a man who has not this unwritten record to which thought and feeling continually recur; and yet there is a constant tendency both in man and society to erase it, — to be occupied, that is, solely with the present, — to live in the present, act for it, and, whatever be the case with the future, never to "look after." A man determined while he lives to assimilate himself to the people with whom he finds himself, to take his cue from them, to fly his kite without the steadying weight of a tail of antecedents, preserves, no doubt, a sense of youth by thus living outside his memory and experience, but it is at the cost of his identity to others, if not to himself. We never know where to have him. Everything is subservient to a restless taste, anxious to conform itself to the current mode. Time has accumulated no treasure for him. The whole paraphernalia of life, former pleasures and pains, with the persons and things that have contributed to them, are judged by taste and the ever-shifting standard of fashion, — that divinity of the present, coldly contemptuous of the past, which, ruling more than dress, equipments, and visiting-lists, tells men what they are to think and feel; so that the things they have once cared for may at any moment be discarded as impertinences, as offenders against the present rule of taste, as so many poor relations intruding on an advanced refinement. For if men do not see old times through a halo of fond memory, the whole thing is a bugbear, — its separate features looming out of a black region of smoke and fog, till the unstable spirit fairly turns its back on the forbidding country that has made it what it is. An elder of this turn, standing amongst his juniors, does not perplex himself with their transient relation to him. He only thinks how he can pass muster and take his stand with them now, unencumbered by prejudice and habit. It is like that dream of a perpetual ascending dizzy progress from stair to stair, where the last stair disappears as we tread upon the next.

And society is apt to show itself as jauntily youthful, as loose from obligations, as oblivious of the past, as careless of association, as individuals. In this temper it is influenced solely by a fastidious principle of selection, a choice of the present, preferable, and popular, over all other considerations, making it a sort of conscience not to be guided by habit or memory, or old opinions, or shadowy presence, — respecting nothing because it stands as it has long stood, but resolved to conform all to the abstract best of which itself is sole judge. We are not advocating a deference for the past which shall interfere with modern convenience, for convenience is often but another word for the means of class advancement. It is merely a question of which influence contributes most to true cultivation, refinement, and elevation,—whether a chain of associations linking present thought with past, assisting men, by whatever means, in the difficult task of realizing things external to themselves, or mere beauty. No doubt beauty, here, as everywhere, has much to say for itself. The poor past is often hard put to it what reason to plead why its memorials should be regarded, why what is unsightly to modern eyes in itself, and a record, perhaps, of evil days, should last; why a phonetic elimination of every awkward and superfluous letter should not be imposed,—why, in fact, time and tradition and a name should sanctify what is ugly, useless, and inharmonious. In the first place, every age has a right to leave some trace of itself just to assert itself; and if it happens to be an age with whose notions of beauty, dignity, or worth we cannot sympathize, that fact does not affect an inherent privilege. The most grotesque likeness of itself it can leave behind is still a picture in Time's portrait-gallery; and it is a breach of natural piety to efface it for any but weighty reasons. This religious aspect of the question is felt strongly enough where taste and fashion do not blind the judgment. Thus, all periods of destruction are regarded with particular hatred when the season of reaction comes, as it surely does; for, in the long-run, men are more agreed in their reverence for a past than in any present question or interest.

The advocates for change often plead religion on their side, as an enthusiast for Gothic architecture will defend his preference on the simple ground that anything else is pagan. Without disputing the point, we would reply, that natural religion was implanted in us prior to revealed, and that it was never intended that the one should outrage the other. However, people who prefer the gratification of a correct eye, or of a theory, to an association, who value a thing more for its conformity to certain laws than for its hidden influences, — for the tale it tells, the scenes it recalls, the names that haunt it, — are not likely to change their liking, and are the last to defer to principles in others which they ignore in themselves. For our part, we would as lief the great memorials of our country were in the hands of the Vandals as in the unrestrained power of what calls itself good taste, and may be, for what we care. We have no sympathy with that pragmatical correctness which, in the assertion of abstract beauty and fitness, would wipe away our records, merely to rid our senses of an anomaly, — which would leave us no past which did not conform to their requirements, and so surely prepare the way for a recriminating future whose reprisals would not leave one stone upon another of our handiwork; so that the disconsolate observer of these desecrations is doubly bereaved, losing his hold of past and future at a stroke. How many æsthetic fingers are tingling now to get into Westminster Abbey and to work their will on those "hideous monuments!" How many think they would be doing God and man service by upsetting the solemn, uncouth, fantastic work of centuries, and turning the outraged pile out of their hands trim and empty of all human association, in the enamelled, spurious youth of restoration! — persuading themselves that the solemn arches and brooding shade would affect the ignorant observer, and tell their story more effectively if no memorial of man were by to distract his attention. But, in fact, eternity needs the contrast of time to most minds for its faintest apprehension; and what fitter portraiture of time than a thousand years of monuments? There are people of taste now using all their efforts to get rid of Laud's north doorway into St. Mary's, because those twisted columns, indeed, the *tout ensemble*, are — we do not dispute it — out of harmony with the building. But surely all expression is attained at some expense of regularity of outline. It is better for Oxford to show traces of having been a centre of thought and action in one of England's most stirring periods than that it should outrage no rule of taste. St. Mary's is more instructive and suggestive as it stands, with this incongruous record of a man, and he a benefactor, who made himself a name, and worked with a purpose, than it could be were the anomaly replaced by a marvel of correct conformity to the main building. A worthy nobleman of our day has pulled down the monument of a family ancestress, the model in her time of beauty, grace, and all conjugal virtues, — a monument set up by an adoring husband, and itself the work of a noted sculptor, — because the cherubs on her tomb had a *faux air* of Cupids and Hymens which interfered with the mediæval repose of restored aisles.

The great work of education, religious and secular, is to enable men to master the idea of time and time's work. If people cannot realize a past, it is a matter of experience that they cannot realize a future. Multitudes live in the present because, out of their own lives, but dimly remembered, they know nothing. "Before my time" embraces all they can conceive of what has been before them. A hundred or a thousand years are all one. It has been asked how many people in England would express a doubt if told that Bonaparte's father was Julius Cæsar; and we fear the true answer would be alike startling and mortifying. We have read lately of a class of school children, well up in their dates, who betrayed in the end an inextricable confusion of ideas between the inspired prophet Samuel and the Bishop of Oxford. It requires more teaching than their circumstances supply to erect anything like an idea, permanent and unfluctuating, of a long course of eventful ages. Every sense, it is true, does something to keep us all *en rapport* with the past. Certain odors awake a vague memory disconnected with anything to remember; and for a moment we feel a weight of intervening years with a sense of some infant joy at the end of them. A quaint, sweet tune of unfamiliar cadences will, if touched off by cunning fingers, convince us of generations of forefathers. But nothing is so all-persuasive as sight; nothing in moral effect is like visible memorials, old people, old cities, old churches, old stones, which are with us to this day. Let the same filial piety extend to and protect them all.

ALLOYS.

WE are in the habit of hearing from the pulpit — and that not now and then, but as a perpetual theme and as a basis of teaching — that men cannot give up the notion of merit, of some inherent positive goodness in themselves; that to be told plainly of the corruption of their nature raises all the venom of the natural man. Without inquiring here how far it is universal with men to care either to *be* good or to be thought so, we do not deny that truth lies somewhere in the charge, though it is often hard to find it in the technical, conventional language exacted by the subject. We have ourselves heard people talk in a very unaccountable way of their deserts and so forth; but we still think it a more difficult matter to believe in human goodness than in the absence of it. People may rebel against a dogma, especially put as some persons put it, but there is something in the idea of any man being positively meritorious which some minds cannot take in. We may and must believe in worthy actions and in relative goodness, but in positive merit we own to seeing a difficulty. It is much more easy for a looker-on to explain away the apparent goodness of those who do the good of the world than frankly to acknowledge it, and honestly, and with heart and understanding, to realize pure *bonâ fide* virtue; and if anything should be a pure and simple essence, virtue should. The work may be valuable, the man may do it well, and we may on this account feel him to be immeasurably better than ourselves; but something always inserts itself between the man and the merit, if we survey the matter at all critically and in the spirit of analysis. No observer, if allowed a full and clear view, can help seeing some alloy in every great and good action whatever, — something to abate the first grand idea. If he is amiable and enthusiastic, he may shut his eyes against what he fears to see; but the cool, unimpassioned temper has seldom far to seek for a qualification, — something to reduce the action from the heroic to the human. Possibly, the preacher may look on this case as a case in point, proving how innate envy and uncharitableness are in man; but we are simply acting on his teaching, working out his theory (which goes far beyond the unreality and imperfection of all human virtue), bringing to the touchstone of individual experience the dogma that merit is an illusion as applied to weak, fallible, complex beings.

All cynicism, however differing in tone, adopts the preacher's language. We cannot, therefore, think it so hard for humanity to disbelieve in human goodness, to see failure and incompleteness in all of it, — something that will not stand a thorough daylight investigation. And does it tell better or worse for the cynic, that it is not scrutiny of others, after all, so much as of self, which is at the bottom of his conclusions? In spite of the apparent denial given to our suspicions by the pretensions of vanity and self-conceit, — those commonest of all human infirmities, — we are disposed to maintain that it is more possible and easy for a mind of any discernment to believe in goodness through other people than through itself. We are very capable of delusion, no doubt; but can any sane man seriously, and in full faith, say to and of himself, — I am good and virtuous, I am good at this moment; not only what I do is good, but I am good in doing it? We do not believe it possible. The same hitch slips in here as in the former case. He repudiates the statement, not only because he is told it is wrong and unchristian, shocking, unprotestant, and heretical to say it, but because he does not in his heart think it, and could not get up the conviction; though we grant that he very possibly considers he makes so excellent an appearance that other people ought to think him good, and, if he is of a hopeful and confiding turn, he supposes that they do, and values himself accordingly. Men do not really get beyond thinking themselves better than they actually are. The assurance of virtue, innate or achieved, is not, we think, compatible with rational humanity. The vainest mortal, the most confident self-deceiver, knows better. When a foolish fellow tells us a long story of his good deeds, — of how he resists this delusion, how he is superior to that temptation, how he devotes himself to a task of pain and difficulty, how his heart is engrossed by noble objects, how he allows himself no rest, how he is fearless, magnanimous, forgiving, — if we had the courage to stop him in mid career, and bid him tell us what he really thought of himself, not as compared with others, but positively, he would stammer out a confession. It would become apparent that, while he was aiming at our reverence, esteem, or admiration, there was more than a doubt at the bottom of his large speaking. Vanity finds food and growth from things wholly different from solid conviction, and that have, indeed, no affinity with it. We lately read of a fantastical German woman who dictated her own *éloge* to an admirer, got him to print it as from himself, then read it as an impartial testimony, and showed extravagant elation and an augmented vanity. By some conjuration, not uncommon in a less degree, she persuaded herself into the notion that she had got at the world's opinion of her.

It is not that in the self-scrutiny, the sifting of evidence, we propose, we shall be driven to condemn our motives wholesale, for people's motives are, as often as not, superior to what the world gives them credit for; but that the mind is conscious of alloy. No actions, if they occupy more than a moment of time, proceed from a single unmixed intention, as all ideal excellence must do; but a whole host of petty, small, snobbish supernumeraries mix themselves up with the professed motive power. Self-approbation, — that support and solace so often promised by a genial philosophy, — is really a delusion. It never gets beyond putting a good face on our actions, bringing the presentable motive into so good a light that we may shuffle the discreditable rivals out of sight; but not — where a man is capable of thought at all — out of mind, nor beyond produceable limits. In fact, a man need not think himself good to be insufferable, — he need only think himself better than his neighbors, and (as we have said) better than he is. Even the Pharisee goes no further than to be thankful he is not as other men are. Pride nourishes itself on comparisons. When the Methodists brought the doctrine of human depravity prominently forward, the then Duchess of

Buckingham, writing to Lady Huntingdon, objected that "It is monstrous to be told you have a heart as sinful as the common wretches that crawl the earth. This is highly offensive and insulting; and I cannot but wonder that your ladyship should relish any sentiment so much at variance with high rank and good breeding." But we are sure, not only that if we could have heard her Grace talk of her noble friends, she would have found a preponderance of alloy in their best actions, but that she would have owned to some in her own case, and that she was a presumptuous heathen through pride of rank rather than from conceit of goodness.

It must be admitted, however, that an irreproachable orthodoxy is found reconcilable with some sort of belief in human goodness, real enough in itself, though perhaps not capable of formal definition; and that belief, not only in good actions, but in a good man, is an elevating belief. The term "good man" is familiar from lips constantly engaged on the fallaciousness of human merit; and those who are willing to show what man can do under high and divine influences, and are jealous of any tone that restricts the capabilities of a renewed will, ransack history and saintly chronicles for examples of pure, unexceptional goodness; and, because they find them, they are very apt to think the former times were better than these. But the truth is, if we are to have perfect examples, we must not hear too much of them, and must get a character fairly away from its contemporaries. It is noticeable that nobody was ever canonized till he was safe from the report of near neighbors, and remembered only for his acts, not with the accompaniment of the daily life in which they were worked out under the observation of eyewitnesses. People who are critical enough of the virtue of their own time are charitable to Roman patriots or Christian ascetics. We have known lovers of the past settle the question by a Scriptural quotation, "There were giants in those days"; and without too curiously testing the logic of the argument, we can believe that other days have encouraged the growth of particular noble qualities more than our own; and in looking back on great men, conspicuous and eminent for one virtue, and constituting our examples, the world is ready to assume that they were everything else besides. But, in fact, who knows what Curtius was in the bosom of his family?

To look on and criticise the active workers of good is, we know, an invidious position. Bacon finely says, "Men must know that in this theatre of man's life it remaineth only to God and angels to be lookers-on." Nevertheless, the critical element is a necessary element, even to secure common fairness. It cannot be amiss that some minds should be observers of facts as such, and not think it a duty to be blind, in certain privileged cases, to deficiencies which so often strike a balance with greatness in a particular line. A man with a sound intellect, a strong will, and one congenial virtue, makes an excellent show and turns into a fine example; but for all this there may be no harm in seeing the reverse side, what lurks in the shade, — the alloy that is so seldom separate from any prominent excellence. The harm lies in its being there, not in an observer seeing it, — in seeing, for instance, in the patient man, apathy; in the energetic man, lack of sympathy; in the public-spirited, cold, natural affections; in the single-minded, crotchetiness and eccentricity; in the conscientious, unreasonableness; in the kind-hearted, indolence; in examples of fidelity, partisanship; in content, sluggishness; in serenity, neglect of duty; in order, self-will and tyranny; in prudence, meanness; in justice, severity; in zeal, intolerance; in warm affections, jealousy and selfishness; in innocence, folly; in sweetness, insincerity; in unworldliness, narrow views; in activity, restlessness; in patriotism, prejudice; in benevolence, want of judgment; in self-sacrifice, obstinacy; in a strict profession, formality; in liberality, display. He is born of the temper of the candid poet, who invoked, not fancy or enthusiasm, but the gift to see things as they are: —

"Come then, fair Truth, and let me clearly see
The minds I paint as they are seen in thee;
To me their merits and their faults impart,
Give me to say, Frail being! such thou art,
And closely let me view the naked human heart."

The eyes of men's minds, as well as of their bodies, see in every variety of focus, — some taking in the fair general effect, some the mechanism of things; and all have their use. There will always be a large proportion of men who judge by effects and results, — who, so long as something good is achieved, and their own ideal advanced, are ready to credit the doer with such a participation of the goodness as lifts him wholly out of the sphere of ordinary natural observation. When once this impression is produced in some minds, submission of the judgment becomes a point of honor, which often grows into an abject subservience not far removed from idolatry. The instinctive student of character is never content with a mere external survey, and thus may often check a generous enthusiasm; but he has his use; he knows that a hundred merely physical and intellectual qualities go to the making of a good man on a great, popular, dazzling scale, but that, after all, motives are the real criterion, and that the best man must be, not he who does the most good, which may depend on other than moral causes, but he who uniformly acts on the highest and purest principles. We have to look into history, chronicles, and newspapers for the one; we must have a close view, and therefore we must look near home, for the other. Mere goodness is that which stands the most minute and severe scrutiny. Greatness, elevation, self-sacrifice, zeal, magnanimity, must have a pedestal, and the lights artistically arranged, to do them justice. They deserve this at our hands, and to be lifted out of the prying of too curious eyes. Only all this respectful caution would not be needed if there were not flaws and alloys, and the risk of very considerable ones.

No doubt the times make a great difference in the exhibition of goodness. Ours are against its more conspicuous displays. A man could once isolate himself, nourish and exercise his particular virtue, leaving the rest to take their chance in a way society does not now allow scope for, and which does not accord with the sway of public opinion. We now exact a harmony of good qualities which unquestionably takes away the glitter and eminence of a character as something to look at.

"A chiel's amang us takin' notes."

Virtue is put upon its p's and q's. And it is this harmony of qualities, allowing no excess even in a virtue, that alone does for close contact and domestic use. As an example to posterity or his fellow-countrymen, or to those who look up to him or down to him from the distance of another class, many a man makes an excellent figure who betrays too much alloy to be relished as a pattern by those who see most of him. But men of all ages must be alike impressed in the presence of consistently pure motives. Here, time and change make no difference. We cannot live in such contact without being aware of it and without reverencing it. Pure motives are things that assert themselves in the long-run and carry the day, though circumstances, or even some want in the man himself, will not allow them to result in remarkable, signally successful action. In the degree that they are pure, they will give — they always have given, and always must give — the highest impression of human goodness that an exact, observant, critical mind can receive, and will constitute, in his case at least, the most influential of all examples.

The Uses of Pathos.

FROM whatever cause, we think it certain that the literature of the present day is deficient in pathos. It makes very little demand on our tears. Perhaps this will hardly be regarded as a subject of regret, now that fashion has set so decidedly in another direction. The race of sentimental young ladies has been laughed out of countenance, or rather they have long ceased to be young ladies at all; while fast girls, who disown romance, have taken their place, and attract or repel, adorn a tale, or point a satire in their stead. Walter Scott, who once possessed the key to youthful hearts, is no longer owned for a magician; he is voted old-fashioned and rather heavy reading. Wordsworth's soundings of the heart of hearts awake no popular response. Society is the present idea of life. The complex workings of a high and often corrupt civilization supersede the more primitive emotions, and they can be portrayed with all degrees of nicety and finish without any invasion of our tender sensibilities. Mr. Thackeray, Mr. Dickens, and Mr. Trollope are in their several ways very clever, amusing, and interesting, and they raise an infinite variety of exciting scenes and images. But we read them in comfortable security. Nobody need be afraid of the red eyes of which our boyhood used to be so ashamed; yet, for this reason, we confess that all of them tell of something that is gone. We miss the old gratified sensation of having been thoroughly stirred up and set to rights, which is, we think, one of the offices of fiction. It was the old Puritanical charge against works of imagination, that they led people to waste their pity and sympathy on fictitious distresses, and left them no tears for actual suffering; but we believe this argument to have been founded on an entire ignorance of the nature of our emotions. We may shed tears over fictitious distresses, and stand dry-eyed in the midst of actual destitution, and in no degree shame our manhood or cast discredit on the author who has charmed us. It is not that we feel less for the one than the other, but that we feel differently; for it is not pain and suffering in themselves that can touch the source of passionate emotion, but something not necessarily of them, though often connected with them. Some touch of the past is essential to make all misery pathetic, — some comparison between former happiness and present pain. People may witness disease, hunger, destitution, and may be keenly alive to them, and earnest to relieve them; but some minor stroke, bringing in strong contrast former ease and joy with present suffering, first excites emotion, — some touch just to make us realize what has been, and to feel the full force of change.

The use of pathos is an indirect one. It must soften and harmonize ourselves before it can benefit others. Its office is to overpower the degrading sense of petty personal worries which haunt and vex, and, what is worse, influence us all so much. Every one is subjected to small annoyances. There is a fret and jar somewhere which makes life's wheels move heavily. If we try to analyze the sense of discomfort, it often admits of no distinct definition; and we are not willing to own ourselves disturbed by so insignificant a cause. The temper suffers; our magnanimity fails us from the very poverty of the grievance. The pathetic, whether seen in actual life or in fiction, is an excellent remedy for this dry, barren dejection. A more generous sentiment suppresses or washes away the rubbish of petty, selfish annoyance. The very thought of the passage of time acts as a corrective of this feeble restiveness under the lesser cares of every-day life. "It will be the same fifty years hence," is a common form of consolation under trivial trials: and Shakespeare gives a pathetic vastness to the idea as he foretells when all time shall be past:—

> "When Time is old and hath forgot himself,
> When water-drops have worn the stones of Troy,
> And blind oblivion swallowed cities up."

Of course, we are not concerned now with emotion as an evidence of real sorrow, but as the symbol of a mixed sensation, bringing warm to the heart the sense of our humanity,—the touch of nature that makes the whole world kin. It is only the reticence of an extreme civilization which hinders a sense of pleasure in this abandonment to feeling. Savages regard tears as a luxury,—as the sign of ecstasy, whether of joy or grief,—and enjoy the sensation, from whatever cause it springs. A Zulu Kafir, for instance, under the rapture of some pungent snuff, exclaimed, "Ah! that was a pinch of snuff; it has brought out the ancient tears that have lived behind my eyes all my life!" Such a stimulant should poetry supply to the civilized man,—tempering, elevating, refining him. We, too, have our ancient tears, whose source lies in the very infancy of memory, which only some subtle touch can draw out,—something sudden, surprising, of the nature of a pang and a wrench, but inducing a sense of calm and relief.

We do not know any two words which express so

well our idea of the pathetic as Tennyson's "divine despair": —

> "Tears, idle tears, I know not what they mean,
> Tears from the depth of some divine despair,
> Rise in the heart and gather to the eyes,
> In looking on the happy autumn fields,
> And thinking of the days that are no more."

Something of the irrevocable — of loss which cannot be restored—enters surely into all pathos, and by contrast sets the mere vexations of the hour at their right level. For this end the loss of some slight good answers often as well as the loss of real essentials to happiness. We accept the trivial severance, so it be only forever, as the type and emblem of a greater. The mind flutters over it, only half conscious of graver partings within reach of our memory if we would look for them. For instance, the poet wanders by a rivulet, and sings a farewell to the burden, —

> "No more by thee my steps shall be,
> Forever and forever."

It is a small matter never to hear again the murmurs of a pleasant stream, but the dim suggestion of similar partings and severances which the words "ever" and "never" like a knell bring along with them, carries the farewell home. It is when memory is the sole link with something past and gone that it puts on the dignity of history and is felt as an influence on our destiny. This is why every event of childhood is so full of meaning to us, —

> "When I was young, — ah! woful when."

The smallest action performed for the last time touches us; the most homely scenes from which we are forever separated have a magic power; feelings transient, momentary, of which we took no note at the time, assume ineffable significance when experience and maturity render their return impossible, and we feel, —

> "Turn whereso'er I may, by night or day,
> The things that I have seen, I now can see no more."

For the moment, the poet here shows us a glimpse of passionate "despair," short-lived though it be. In the unavailing longings of his immortal ode we realize something of the meaning of time and death. There is a well-known passage in testimony to the English Bible, from the pen of a distinguished convert to Rome, which owes its inspiration and passion to the same cause, — that is, to intense and bitter remembrance of a stage of life all astir and beautiful with thought, feeling, and action, but past beyond recall. "It lives on the ear like a music that can never be forgotten, — like the sound of the church-bell which the convert hardly knows how he can forego"; and yet it is because he had foregone it in his own deliberate intention forever that he wrote so movingly and well. In the same way gratitude has its pangs and becomes pathetic, as in Burns's Lament for Glencairn. The sense of loss and irrevocable change may exist in feeling, though not in fact, is in the home-sickness of Cowper's school-boy,—"with what intense desire he wants his home." It gives the power to those words of Jane Eyre, "Now I thought." It is the motive of all the pathos in "Adam Bede," whether the author speaks in his own person or by his characters. We see it in poor Flora Macdonald's "Ay, there it is, Mr. Waverley." It is the irrevocable resolve in Othello which shakes us as he addresses himself to his purpose, "Put out the light, and then put out the light." It gives a sense of eternity to pain in his "insupportable and heavy hour." It may, we think, be traced in all the simpler motives and impulses to emotion, as when masters of the pathetic describe anguish, sickness, suspense, death, and bereavement; but it is not well to push a view too far.

Contrast of some sort,—something coming upon us as a surprise,—is, however, essential. To persons new to physical suffering, the contrast between disease and health, between the condition of humanity as it is and as it ought to be, may suffice to excite a passionate emotion without further insight. Again, a desolate hopelessness, by some unexpected turn of fortune suddenly changed to joy, affects us as keenly as the reverse might do. There are wonderful examples of this from a source too sacred to be included in our examples. It is as an elevating and important, not as the sole element of passionate emotion, that we give so large a place to the irrevocable, — to the fact that nothing can be recalled, nothing can be reversed as though it had never been, making us in some slight degree realize the burden of the past. Such thoughts must bring a certain pang and heart-ache, just pain enough to make us sensible of an effort and a summoning of our powers, — an effort as essential to all the highest forms of pleasure as to all thought deserving the name, and which, when made, has an immediate cheering and salutary effect on the spirits and temper. Pathos, then, is the "timely utterance" which gives relief to more thoughts than it knows of, for no doubt the cares which contract most brows and drive the smile from most faces are cares which find no expression in tears, and for which such tears are often the best remedy.

For whatever reason, we believe there are few things the world sets more value on than its tears, — not individual tears, which, we admit, are apt to meet with scanty sympathy, but the visible, tangible evidence of a universal heartache, however transient. They have a remedial and atoning power that the scorners of sentiment never allow for. When ladies, and especially gentlemen, cry, we grant they should be careful of their company. Society is a soberer, and puts a veto on such indulgence which all sensible, strong-minded folks, whatever their natural temperament, acquiesce in. But a nation (as distinct from society) allows itself a freer scope, and adopts another standard. Its tears are an equivalent for more sorrows and losses than can be well imagined; indeed, we hardly know any calamity which is not more than compensated for in our imagination by being thoroughly regretted and grieved over. Take all history, and measure its tales of colossal loss, its catastrophes, and broken hopes by the tears shed for them, and if only they flowed readily enough, and were commensurate with the occasion, we find our minds satisfied and at ease. It is only those unwept, unhonored, and unsung whose fate we pity and yearn over. One pang of which tears are the expression, one twinge passing through the nation with an electric shock, satisfies us of so many things. It implies that the lost good has been valued and enjoyed, which is much, — that it has been missed, which is far more. What else can an earthly good do for us? What more can our heroes and saints expect from us? And with regard to fictitious sorrows, it is untold how much more comfortable and virtuous, how much more conscientiously free from blame, the English public feels with regard to slavery, since it wept collectively over the sorrows of Uncle Tom; and, in a more restricted sense, a good many of our injustices towards a past generation are atoned for by the same method in our reception of Adam Bede. There may be some sham in it all, as in all general movements there must be; but we hold that the world is always better and more *human* for these deviations from its ordinary callous indifference of aspect, and that it is the part of literature to supply this healthful influence.

But the face of society is not friendly to outbreaks of feeling. It is the general complaint that even the young are hard and calculating, with an eye to careless jollity on the one hand, and the main chance on the other; and our popular writers do not do much to counteract the prevailing tendency. Mr. Dickens, we admit, has his own idea of pathos, but too far removed from our own,—too remote from experience or from our conception of the possible,—to find response, much less to influence popular feeling. We are not sure that the present system of serials and monthly chapters, all of which must contain present amusement whether they tell a story or not, have not a great deal to answer for on this head. The system is essentially degrading to the imaginative faculty.

The writer writes and the reader reads under wholly different conditions from those in which author and reader stood in the days of Richardson and Walter Scott. Aim and influence must be shaken by this disjointed, desultory, broken utterance. The old idea of subjugation under an author is lost; the words "spell" and "thraldom," which used to express it, have no meaning as applied to our present literature. Fancy "Old Mortality" issued in twenty-four green-backed numbers, or the "Bride of Lammermoor" coming out in the "Cornhill." People must be in very exceptional circumstances to be tempted to write a romance or a moving picture of life now-a-days. There is so little sympathy for the state of feeling which prompts such efforts that it would seem an author must have nothing to do with society, — must even be removed by some impassable barrier from its blandishments, — before he can make his way to our deeper selves. It would seem, but we know it is not so, and the genius has only to appear and shine out amongst us to show the fallacy of our fears, and restore the pathetic to its right and natural place amongst us.

CHOICE.

THERE is surely a benignant fallacy in the notion that possesses men of their unlimited powers of choice. The language of courtesy assumes, of all persons with whom one has polite relations, that they have a constant choice of eligible alternatives. Men are supposed to choose their wives, — even young women their husbands, — to choose, that is, from among many. A gentleman of pure African descent, educated, but coal-black, was one of a company where the position of the Prince of Wales became the topic of conversation. Others descanted on the more brilliant features of his lot. Pity, evidently genuine, was the sole feeling inspired in the negro listener. The Prince had only six ladies to choose from; he spoke as if, in his own more fortunate case, the world lay all before him where to choose. And Charles Lamb, in his splenetic paper on the insolence of young married women, claims for the bachelor such width and continual exercise of conscious choice, that he holds him as rejecting every single woman to whom he does not make an offer of his hand. It contributes to people's happiness and self-respect to have a sense of wide, active choice. The slightest conscious restriction hampers and irritates; but except in moral choice,— the election between good and evil perpetually carried on within us,—with which we are not here engaged, —it is an effort of mind which ordinary life, sensibly conducted, offers fewer opportunities for than are assumed. Men are not often brought face to face with an important choice, and in fact live very contentedly under obligations that leave no room for one. The more people exercise reason and judgment, the less choice they perceive themselves to have in matters of every-day experience. Thus, if a man has to furnish his house, it indefinitely limits his choice to know what he wants; and good taste still further restricts his field; for choice implies some degree of acceptance, or, at least, toleration, of two or more objects. The reason why some people hang suspended in helpless uncertainty before a hundred possibilities, thinking that they are choosing, is constantly that they cannot collect their thoughts or master the position sufficiently for the preliminaries of a reasonable judgment. The moment this is formed, it is not that they choose, but that they awake to the fact that there is only one rational decision open to them, and that all the rest are mere gross and palpable temptations.

In the ordinary conduct of life, it is constantly found what meaningless phrases are choice of society, choice of a profession, choice of time, place, and habits; though it softens the bitterness of necessity to have a lip familiarity with the words, whether unconsciously, as adopting the prevailing idiom, or consciously, like Beau Tibbs, who chose to live in a garret for the sake of the view. In choosing a wife or a husband, the affections, in a right state of things, constitute this compulsion, rendering the idea of choice irrelevant. The heart does not ring with a full, clear sound whenever there can be dispassionate choice in this matter. "Chance," and not choice, Dr. Johnson says, "gives a man a partner whom he prefers to all other women, without any proof of superior desert." So it was meant to be. The Cœlebs engaged in choosing a wife is a prig, or the victim of a hard necessity; and the woman who, in our state of society, has two lovers to choose from at the same moment, in spite of the glory attributed to the position by novelists and young ladies, is probably a flirt, or has behaved like one, and has more cause for shame than triumph. The eminence is won at some expense of simple honesty and honor. And even where there is ample excuse, as in the case of beauties and heiresses, the power of choice among many is so contrary to what is right and natural that choosing here proverbially means choosing the worst.

In cases which seem to depend solely on our own will, it is often curious to see how choice flies us, — how some unexpected hinderance or defect in ourselves balks expectation. A man, for example, of a literary turn, with leisure, independence, and all the necessary qualifications, wishes to put his thoughts and experience in some durable shape. His information is general, his observation has been wide, — he has only to choose a subject for his book. But to his own surprise he finds that he has no choice. One subject, and that he is aware not a popular subject, one he cannot hope to persuade many to care for, is already master of the field and will keep foremost. His thoughts have a bent apart from the inclination of the whole man. He feels as if he could not help himself, and the idea of choice is postponed to the next attempt. Criticism always goes on the assumption of free choice on the part of the criticised. Thus, the plot of a tale or drama is exposed for its errors, short-comings, absurdities. The work has merit, but the author ought to have chosen his incidents, his characters, his situations, with more judgment; more pains, more thought, more weighing and deliberation, would have mended everything, and set all right. The author possibly agrees with every word, but he feels as if he had had no choice. The story and the personages arranged themselves somehow. He does not see how he could have managed differently. No writer is quite, and in every sense, master of his pen. And even in conversation it is often curious to observe how hard a matter choice is. There are generally one or two topics that circumstances bring uppermost, which a man, or a circle, naturally hits upon first. If anything renders these natural self-suggesting topics unsuitable or unsafe, how hard is the choice of a subject, how distractedly and blindly the mind feels about for some substitute, and how importunately will the obvious but discarded theme obtrude itself again and again, till there seems nothing in the world to say but just what ought not to be said; while it is observable that, once in this predicament, it is chance and not choice that gets us out of it! Even in such matters as the scene of an excursion or the naming of a child, where our field of selection seems literally without bounds, we presently find a thousand limitations to our assumed liberty, till we feel hemmed in, and are amazed at the smallness of our choice after all.

Those are not the most comfortable people to live with who will not recognize these restrictions, — who regard private life as a theatre for the constant exercise of choice in domestic fundamentals, and will not consent to consider any decision permanent or lifted from the balance of reconsideration, — who admit no precedents, who reflect each morning at what hours they shall eat and drink, who bring upon the tapis as an ever new subject for consideration and choice how the day is to be spent, what church they shall go to, what newspaper they shall take in.

> "He lives by rule who lives himself to please," —

and to be able to regard some things as certain and removed from the thought of change and choice is as necessary for the comfort of social communities as for the individual. For the exercise of choice ought to be, and is to most people, a fatigue, an effort of the mind; and to be always frittering it away in settling matters which best settle themselves, is to become tedious, eccentric, frivolous, thus vitiating the discernment for those real occasions of choice which some time or other present themselves to every man. The state of indecision in which some people live may be called a morbid exercise of choice. There are persons who never seem to have quite made up their minds which leg to stand upon, — who deliberate in an agony of choice when not a grain's weight depends on the decision, on the question what road to walk on, what chair to sit down upon, what bundle of hay to munch first. The way to cure this disease is by external applications, — that is, by feigning a choice though there be none, — by pronouncing authoritatively for port or claret, the leg or the wing, while the soul and intellect are still all in tumult and confusion about the matter.

To all appearance, men are allowed a wider field of choice than formerly, and it opens to them earlier. At one time, parents chose everything for their children, from a profession to a wife, perhaps laying their life out for them before they were born. Now, choice is recognized as an educator; and, in fact, it is a great part of training to teach how to choose and what are fit subjects for choice. One does not know which is most mischievous, — never to allow a choice at all, or to force responsibility prematurely before the mind can command the data for a true decision, when the crude judgment must come to a conclusion either on no reason at all, or a wrong one. It often happens to a young man, because he is promising, to have to choose his line too early; and, for ultimate success, he can scarcely be visited by a greater misfortune. Precocious talent, combining with circumstances, sometimes produces a youth of brilliant maturity remarkable for seeming vigor of choice, and the end is almost certainly a manhood of indecision and failure. Ability to choose is power and genius. There is, indeed, something godlike in the constant, wise exercise of free will and selection, — so much so that the supremest instances in sacred or profane story of wise choice cannot keep up the strain. That mythical personage, the true hero, is ever choosing his course. Great captains and statesmen, however really victims of accident, are popularly supposed, — as holding our destinies in their hands, — to be doing the same; and it may be granted that the degree in which men exercise choice, and the objects on which they exercise it, make the difference between great and little lives. But the hinderances to this exercise, in most minds, are innumerable. Habit, prejudice, foregone conclusions, are, of course, among the first of these. People are so slow to perceive their responsibilities, to catch the critical moment when choice was open to them, that the course they are in carries them past it unobserved through its own impetus. It is a curious and not always pleasant speculation to look back and note when those occasions presented themselves where we might have exercised a choice to which we were blind at the time. No doubt this very preparedness is a sign of genius, and distinguishes one soul from another. In fact, whatever afterthought may tell us, no man can be said to have had a choice if he did not know that he had one; and persons in bondage to prejudice and circumstances never do. There is even a fine, dogged, half-stupid sense of duty which sometimes holds people in this unconsciousness. They go on in a course not really obligatory, because it never occurs to them that they have a choice. It has been argued that, whatever the issue of the contest, the Americans had no choice but to go to war; that there are losing games which must be played at whatever cost; and that all the blood and suffering were consequently inevitable, because a nation cannot stop in its course and face a critical decision. The poor rustic, with his nine shillings a week, never recognizes that he has any other choice than the proverbial Hobson's, — his present wages or nothing, — or, at any rate, his ill-paid labors or enlisting; therefore, he *has* no choice. He never sees the moment, which does present itself to such as can discern it, of escape from drudgery to a new life of change and adventure. He knows nothing of the choice that education and intercourse would bring before him, revealing to his quickened capacity an alternative which, until he is fit for it, he had, perhaps, best not attempt to realize.

We have spoken of indecision, — of persons helpless when called upon in the most insignificant matters to make an instantaneous choice; but we cannot, therefore, sympathize with some who value themselves on their readiness in this particular, — who boast of always being able to make up their minds on the spot. It is very pleasant to be able to settle everything on the instant, if we settle right, but judgment and deliberation have their parts to play in our affairs. When we have to choose at all, it is seldom that all our grounds for choice lie on the surface or immediately within reach. We do not observe that it is the fullest minds that find their way to a choice quickest; nor does it always prove that it was the best choice because the chooser remains satisfied with it. Indeed, it is one property of learning and knowledge to hold men's judgment in suspense until every contingency has been passed in review. Such habitual promptness as reason sanctions is, however, indispensable to those crowning efforts of rapid decision, — that is, choice of alternatives, — which we call presence of mind, and without which courage is often useless. In a great fire, a lady, conscious of having much valuable property in her room, rushed back to save what she could. There was money, there were jewels, and other fine things. By desperate exertions she reached the spot; and at length emerged from the smoke and flame panting and breathless, convulsively clasping in her hands, — a small-tooth comb. The power to choose in the last moment had deserted her, leaving us to speculate on what habits of mind might have helped her to turn an impulse of courage and daring to better account. To know how to choose, then, is a triumph of natural powers, of thought, reason, and self-discipline. To know when to choose marks discretion and good sense. The very effort of choice gives strength and nerve to the mind; yet a prudent man will scarcely desire unlimited opportunities for it, — will readily admit that to see where there is no choice and frankly to accept the inevitable is often a mark of the highest wisdom, — and will gladly recognize the interference of chance and accident, even in those actions which are considered as particularly subjects of choice. For, after all, choice is a thing to fear. There is something irrevocable in it; it is not only in marriage or the wedding-gown that choice is once for all. An important decision, once come to and acted upon, cannot be wholly reversed. The looker-on does not know why, but nothing can be absolutely undone in this life. Persons jealous to shape their own course, who turn their backs upon obvious or natural influences, and choose for themselves, assume a responsibility which, while it does not remove them from the operations of chance, seems to change it into an austere, unfriendly power, visiting upon them every mistake of conduct, every failure of judgment.

To them chance never appears the indulgent harmonizer and reconciler, the gentle Providence which it not seldom shows itself to such as own their inability to direct their own course, and willingly submit to the guidance of events or to the sway of circumstances.

One's Own Way.

A GOOD many qualities and propensities are visited with universal censure, which people would not abuse so much if there were any danger of their warning being taken literally, or, indeed, having much effect at all. The moralist habitually indulges in a strain of animadversion, secure that the instinct which he denounces is too deeply fixed and ingrained for any chance of his words producing much effect, and would be frightened to be taken too much at his word. This is a fact which needs to be constantly kept in mind. A great deal of the best teaching is only valuable under the tacit understanding of this resistance in our nature to its indiscriminate reception; so that whatever the words of the teacher may seem to imply, extermination is not really contemplated, only a pruning of excess, bringing the quality in question under due subordination. Thus selfishness is unreservedly denounced, because the instinct of self-love is really invulnerable. In like manner, the young are warned against the love of dress in terms which seem to counsel an utter disregard of the graceful and becoming, because it may be safely assumed that no words will ever persuade them not to set themselves off to advantage, and that we might as well preach to the roses as to the virgin that loveth to go gay, to abandon all care for shape and texture and color at our bidding. Amongst these qualities, only evil in excess, — and beneficial, and even indispensable, short of this excess, — which have yet been the object of constant reprobation and a theme for reproof and warning without end, is the love of one's own way. Divines, moralists, and poets, all conspire, as far as words go, to quench this lesser development of the spirit of liberty, as though love of one's own way implied wilfulness, hardness of heart, insubordination, all that is ungentle and unlovable. But it is, after all, only seeming, — experience teaches them quite another lesson. The poet, for all his sweet testimony to the yielding, submissive spirit which moves through life, —

> "Com' animal gentil che non fa scusa
> Ma fa sua voglia della voglia altrui,"

must himself be free as air before he can indite a line. The moralist does not find his thoughts at his command or his judgment in working order while under the control of others, — he must be his own master before he can impose his salutary restraints on mankind, — and the divine is probably the most self-willed of the three, only after a method peculiarly his own. He must have his time, his thoughts, his movements entirely at his own disposal, subject to none but voluntary distractions and self-imposed rules, before he can dictate, with sufficient force to be effective, his arguments for an implicit subjugation of the will to the Church and to the world. One and all know quite well — or might know, from themselves and their own requirements — that something of one's own way is as necessary to the intellectual and even moral faculties as light and air to vegetation. It is the abuse, the excess, they are warring against, so far as their teaching is wise and good, — not the desire itself, which is simply the consciousness of a separate existence, and the impulse to preserve and assert this individuality. It is the repugnance of a free agent to lapse into an instrument, a tool, a machine. Of course always to assert the will is insubordination and anarchy, but never to give it play is bondage. The question is, where to find the golden mean.

Surely no one will have too much of his own way who is careful never to infringe on the rights of others, and who is ready to admit that every individual in the world has such rights, and ought to be allowed a sphere for their exercise. Always, and as a rule, to yield, is to encourage others in a tyranny which is bad for them. This is known to be the case in religious, or quasi-religious, communities, where abnegation of the will is strongly and technically enforced, and where a domineering spirit sometimes gains a frightful ascendency. What is so bad for one cannot be good for the rest who seek to throw on their neighbor an inalienable responsibility. But we are growing too serious, and, in so doing, departing from our limits, which strictly confine us to the minute domestic phase of the great subject of freedom, — that phase, however, in which it affects the bulk of mankind. Political freedom — that is, our own way on the grandest collective scale — comes home to us only on stated occasions, and, to most people, never as a practical question at all. Even independence seems limited to householders, fundholders, and the elder and privileged classes; but the freedom we mean has an interest for us all and touches every one's daily life. It develops powers, — it forms the character. The possession or the want of it strikes the balance between existences which, to the casual observer, stand on the two extremes of prosperous and adverse. Many an anxious and laborious life is tolerable, and is carried through with a cheerfulness and elasticity exciting constant admiration, because the weight is laid where it can be easiest borne, — an adjustment which people can generally best do for themselves. A sense of power comes with difficulties met and overcome by our own resources, directed in our own way; while, on the other hand, there are lives which seem peculiarly exempt from the ordinary trials of life, vexed with no great cares, secure of the main blessings, surrounded, perhaps, by the luxuries others want, but which cannot be enjoyed because of the consciousness of some external power which interferes with every natural spring of action, makes every step compulsory, and renders all seeming choice a dead letter. And this, again, accounts for many a dogged, passive, indifferent manner, provoking, perhaps, in the undiscerning looker-on, — who assumes that pleasant circumstances should necessarily bring pleasure, — all sorts of disparaging and unjust surmises. It is here that two instincts come in contact which are often confused, but really distinct, — the love of one's own way, which, in reason, we defend; and the love of influence and love of rule, that is, the passion for marking out other people's way for them. This last is, indeed, so often engendered by an uninterrupted career of one's own way — a state of things leaving no growth for the sympathy which arises out of fellow-feeling — as to give some color to the confusion. There are men who devote their lives to the cause of political liberty, and yet see no inconsistency in imposing their own private peculiarities as a law on others; who prescribe their own strictly personal, and perhaps eccentric, habits on their children and dependants, and think they do all that is required in saying, "I ask no more from them than I do myself." They are quite unconscious that an act, perhaps indifferent in itself, is pleasure to them because it is the offspring of their own fancy, because it is a whim, because it fits in with their idiosyncrasy; and, therefore, by the same rule, may be disagreeable to others whose insides, mental and corporeal, are differently constituted. Such men, without knowing it, are perpetually stirring up an atmosphere of irritation around them. Every time their back is turned there is some little explosion, a petty indemnification for a petty tyranny; for it is certain, — we will not say of all races, for, as Mrs. Gamp very justly remarks, "There may be Rooshians and there may be Prooshians," and we do not pronounce upon them, — but it is certain that all members of the Anglo-Saxon race will take it out in some way or other, if they are thwarted of what they feel their legitimate share of their own way.

Among the surest recipes to be well loved, well obeyed, well served, is to be careful not to interfere with this inalienable privilege. Even with our servants, if they know their business, it is best to confine our orders to things being well done without interfering minutely with times and modes. Any one who knows by observation or experience what it is to be managed or dictated to, to have his movements followed, his time in indifferent matters regulated for him, — who has felt actually, or by sympathy with some sufferers, these moral gyves and fetters precluding all escape from a predominant will, — should allow his butler or his housemaid scope, not only for the exercise of their independent reason, but for some little caprice of will, on the ground that every human being ought to have an arena of action in which he can work after his fancy, and do things in a certain fashion and order, because it is his way. Service — and most relations, whether of friendship, affection, or duty, have something of the nature of service in them — means subjecting our wills in important matters. It is not only hirelings who have to submit their inclinations to an external control: husbands, wives, children, friends, subjects, must all do it in the natural course of things. But all service is light or galling not so much from the amount of labor and the great tasks and concessions required, as from the circumstances under which they are accomplished. Everything depends on whether we have a sense of liberty with them or of bondage; and needless interference with our mode of action, with our own system of adapting our work to our temperament and character, is this bondage. We say "we," but it is not a personal question. We are pleading for the weak,— for such as cannot help themselves. A man who has found his place in the world has not often much to complain of on this head, though there are exceptional cases. He may now and then be taken possession of by some meddling spirit, who, either from fussy affection, want of tact, jealousy, or love of management, lifts him off his feet as it were, and gives him a momentary taste of subjection; but his keen irritation at the situation shows how little he is used to interference. It is his own fault if he lives a victim to such trammels. In the main, he has enough of his own way. But there are many over whom circumstances predominate, and who live and die under the dominion of a strong will,—whose best gifts are dwarfed, who never have a chance, who never fairly taste of life, and who are incapacitated for their place in it from being the victims of a life-long, minute subjection of the will. In these cases—and all must know some instances to the point—women are generally the sufferers, and women the tyrants; the first from the weakness of their sex, which, while it keeps them ever fretting under the yoke, does not give them strength to cast it off; and the other, from the greater aptitude for frivolous, unceasing interference which the feminine nature, allied to a strong will, possesses. Men are greater bullies than women; but they have not the same eye for surveillance. If they do attempt it, the mischief and the misery are indeed at their highest.

A certain yoke of general superintendence is of course necessary for youth. The words "training," and "education," imply it; and children may have their way marked out for them, even in trifles, without any irritating sense of dictation. Indeed, they are conscious of a general need of guidance, and are happier with it. But even children should, within a limited sphere, be intrusted with some choice of their own way, in which their own reason and experience should be their only teachers. This is why school, with all its dangers, is often better for a boy than an ultra-careful home, where perhaps he is answerable to a watchful mother for the outlay of each penny of his pocket-money, and stands reproved for every damage to his playthings. We are very far from wishing for the young of either sex to be allowed too much of their own way; but it is one of the secrets of wise management to manage as little as possible, and never to interfere unnecessarily, or in trifles and things of little moment. If we rule, it is best not to show that we rule them.

In one sense, this secret is a wonderful economist; for one of the cheapest and at the same time most effectual ways of making people happy, especially where pleasure is the avowed pursuit, is simply to leave them to do as they like and choose their own way of enjoying themselves. To go where you like and do what you like, instead of what other people like, or what is expected from you, often brings a sense of relief, of holiday, of lightness and jollity, which no amount of show, no lavish expense can in the least counterbalance. Young people, and old people too, often only need this to enjoy the most complete relaxation of which they are capable; and yet this is precisely what the managing temper, prolific of plans and programmes, cannot and will not understand. It is the presence or absence of this spirit of dictation which makes some homes pleasant, others irksome. The same people in the same combinations may meet in both, and yet not know themselves or each other in the opposing atmospheres.

Perhaps it explains our meaning of "one's own way," while it obviates the charge of selfishness to which some expressions may have subjected it, that while it alone gives a sense of ownership in the things about us, it extends that sense to the greatest number with every gratifying circumstance of possession, and yet without interfering with others' rights.

Mere legal ownership, under the check of an overmastering will, goes very little way towards real proprietorship. The strong will which takes the headship assigns, disposes, apportions, according to its own notions, till the saying come true, — and not only a man's land, his house, his child, his coat, but even his soul is not his own. But where every member of a family has his free development, the same thing belongs to a dozen different people. The master, the mistress, the children, the servants, all say *my* and *our* indiscriminately, — and with reason, for what is ownership but the sense of doing what you like, exercising your will upon the thing in question? And this can be done, and is done, where people live happily together, without a moment's infringement of the more absolute class of rights. Nor, indeed, can we feel at ease, even as an acquaintance, much less as a friend, without sharing this privilege of possession, and all that sense of ownership which lies hid in "being at home," — without having established some rights, imprinted our will on some corner, some nook, some seat, where we may have the pleasant security of being allowed "our own way."

Want of Money.

If one slight change were made in the circumstances of the mass of society, what an astounding effect would be produced! And yet our supposed case could not be put in any startling form. It is only that, instead of people, as a rule, having less money than they want, — less than seems necessary for the working out and fit fulfilment of the duties and pleasures of their position, — all had just a little more than enough. It appears a simple idea, and pleasant as it is simple. It is no unreasonable stretch of the imagination, — just a little surplus for everybody, sufficient to make all ends meet, and a little over; yet, in fact, it would turn the world upside down, and that in a week's time. Want of money is the principle of moral gravitation, — the only power, as we are constituted, strong enough to keep things in their places. It is this shortness and dearth which our supposed change would remove, —

this perpetual deficiency, this constant hitch, this all but ineffectual struggle to keep above water, — which maintains the world's stability, and saves us from perpetual change and dissolution. It is the difference between a close fit and even a small surplus and excess which alone keeps men to the work of their lives. It is the one stern cure for restlessness, — the potent guide to consistency which nobody can evade. All labor, whether of mind or hand, would be spasmodic and intermittent without it. It is the only *must* in a free country that men have to obey all their lives. If people had once money enough to stop in their career, to turn round, to look about them, to debate matters, to try experiments, to indulge fancies, to yield to disgusts, society would come to a dead-lock; there would be first universal change, and then nobody can guess what. But, to speak generally, nobody has enough; for in a question of this sort the really rich are so minute a minority as not to count, and it is most happy that it is so.

Indeed, without going into the case speculatively, nobody does wish for universal wealth. This moderate rise from a little short of enough to a little above it, from straitness to ease, is a wish that people instinctively reserve for themselves and their friends. It is only for self and a chosen few that such aspirations are formed as we find condensed in the Scotchman's prayer for a modest competency: — "And, that there may be no mistake, let it be seven hundred a year paid quarterly in advance." We know well enough, without consulting the political economists, that it would be highly inconvenient if all the sons of toil, by whom we live, had, even according to their own limited ideas, a remunerative, generous return for their labors, and were thus enabled to stop and deliberate, and change their calling when weary of it. Want of money is an external force necessary to the world's stability, but which our reason is slow honestly to recognize in cases nearly concerning ourselves. It is a spur no one is willing to believe indispensable to himself. To each man it is a superhuman effort of humility to believe that pecuniary necessities are essential to his going through life with decent credit, — that he is incapable of getting good and happiness out of a full purse. But we cannot help seeing that, in the case of many another man, it is well for "want to be his master," — that there are people who were patient, humble, striving, laborious, contented, under a narrow fortune, but whom money has completely upset, on whom it has wrought like the insane root.

These admissions are necessary, and we have to repeat such arguments often, to reconcile ourselves to the weight and sadness which this all but universal condition of humanity induces in the social atmosphere. Even passing through the streets, how many wrinkled brows and careworn physiognomies we meet which we learn to trace to this one source! The poor have no skill at disguising their anxieties. These are written, in large characters on their whole bearing, and the very title we give them reveals the source of their anxieties; but others who have learnt the graceful art of concealment, — who wear a social smile as part of a liberal education, — how often we catch their faces betraying, as it were, some process of mental arithmetic, as though some sum were being cast up within which will not give the wished-for answer. It is said that you cannot overhear Americans talk for two minutes without the word "dollars" coming in. In the old country it is rather the want of the dollar, or its equivalent, which impresses itself on the aspect of things, — not, we must own, by any evidences of squalor, but by the general carefulness and anxious deliberation that is the prevailing characteristic of a crowd. Imagine for an instant the change from this gravity, deepening often into gloom, which would be apparent in the air and look of our streets, if every one we met had found himself that morning with ten pounds in hand! For the extended wealth we are imagining is not large possessions. We do not say, with the Roman, "that man is rich who can maintain an army," but he who is absolutely easy in his circumstances, whatever they are, and knows no care about money.

When we speak of want of money being a universal disease, we imply that it is a respectable one, and belonging to the responsible portion of the community. It is not only jovial Falstaffs who can find no remedy for this consumption of the purse. Nor do we confine ourselves by any means to poverty in its strictest sense; though, of course, where there is debt and embarrassment it is felt at its worst. Careful fathers of families, prudent tradesmen, are, we know, thinking of ways and means, — the dull eye, the heavy tread betray them. Pious rectors, painstaking curates, — it is not parish, or sermon, or speculative thought alone which chastens and subdues their outer man to such seeming conformity with their calling. Plodding students, hard-working lawyers, devoted young doctors, are seldom quite absorbed in their respective cases. On all and each there is a superadded care, — a worry that does not belong to their work. The traces of a struggle are upon them all. The people who have not to think about money as an anxious subject, who have no care about it, who are never seriously checked by it, who are not periodically kept awake by it, whose reveries are not tinged by it, for themselves, or those they care for like themselves, are so few, compared with the whole community, that they need not be taken into the account. If any man at ease in his own circumstances does not know the feeling, it is that his exceptional position, the isolation of his prosperity, stints his sympathy. All people who can feel for others and are therefore admitted into confidences, or who more likely understand without any spoken confidence at all, find this a weight, — an abiding though probably salutary sadness. How many young spirits they see prematurely depressed by this want, — it may be the consequence of their own folly! How many manners, tempers, peculiarities may be interpreted by it! How many people are dull, or proud, or unsociable from the secret irritation of want of money! How many bright intelligences are diverted from their highest development from the same cause! We are not quarrelling with things as they are, — we have asserted, on the contrary, that it is all-essential to the world's well-being; but nevertheless this painful side of the question does appear to exist. We know so many people who seem as if they would be the better for easy circumstances and a relaxation from care.

However, human shoulders are made to bear heavy burdens. If we could see into the inner anxieties of many a cheerful exterior, we should wonder how the cheerfulness could be maintained. But, in fact, the universality of the evil makes it bearable. There is a sustaining, inspiriting reliance on fellow-feeling, pervading every circle, though scarcely realized till it is missed; as it is missed in the presence of obtrusive wealth, — wealth that makes itself felt like a barrier, either by vulgar pride of purse, contempt of small expense, or by the cool assumption that want of money in all its consequences is no evil, and is not hard to bear, and involves no real privation. There is a certain insolence of satiety, peculiarly irritating to the spirit which feels its wings, but may not use them. And yet such people have something to say for themselves, in whatever way they make themselves offensive. Perhaps nothing should console us more for our friends' or our own want of money than the extraordinary uses to which people who have it put their superfluity. It often seems difficult to get pleasure out of money, though, in the abstract, nothing seems so easy. Speculation may be a foolish luxury, and extravagance is undoubtedly wrong, but they are both more intelligible than the creditable methods some rich men hit upon for the disposal of vast sums, which are often curiously like throwing money into the river or burying it. The tricks some men play with the surface of their estates are of this sort to the unsympathizing looker-on. The passion for earthworks, for displacing stones or soil, for levelling or hollowing, raising mounds, diverting streams, and so forth, — all on a scale commensurate with their fortune, — are very like contrivances to get rid of money. There are sermons in all stones; and though our eye is not insensible to the gratification of an unbroken length of granite, we must regard a monolith — for thousands of years the supreme achievement of wealth — as an emphatic preacher of content to the poor man. And even when the rich enter into more intelligible expense, they seem to have to spend, not in proportion to the thing aimed at, but to their means. If a rich man adds a wing to his house, by a certain law he has to spend five times as much upon it as we can understand by the results. He gets no more pleasure, scarcely more effect out of it, than where the same thing is done by others who have to think of money at every turn. Perfect finish and completeness enormously affect the whole outlay, but not, to the same degree, the imagination. Not many people, it is clear, get much enjoyment out of a large fortune. Who does not feel that he could manage one better than the actual possessor? Now, in the mere question of buying, how few can indulge in the delicious pleasure of buying, — not of *spending*, that comes of itself without active steps on our part, but of *buying*, —

visibly exchanging our money for what we can hold in our hand! How few can safely buy a thing because they fancy it, not because it cannot be done without! But the amusement of buying evidently palls where there is no difficulty. What men may have any time for the asking they often don't care to have at all. An acquisition to a poor man is a sort of conquest, like that black-letter folio immortalized by Charles Lamb, to procure which the "old brown suit was made to hang on six weeks longer." Then, when rich people do seem to enjoy their money, we often don't like their way of doing it. Persons who know nothing of poverty are sometimes cold, hard, and uninteresting. They betray a barren complacency, and care for their possessions chiefly as giving them what others want, — for making them enviably singular. They are consequently extremely jealous of all general benefits to mankind, — just as a good many people quarrelled with railroads because they deprived them of the power of travelling faster than other folks. However, we will not pursue this part of our theme further. Moralizing is so easy and so obvious, and yet nobody feels quite honest while he indulges in it. As we write, Johnson's confessions on this point will obtrude themselves: — "When I was running about this town a very poor fellow, I was a great arguer for the advantages of poverty; but I was at the same time very sorry to be poor. Sir, all the arguments which are brought to represent poverty as no evil show it to be evidently a great evil. You never find people laboring to convince you that you may live very happily upon a plentiful fortune." And Sydney Smith spoke in the same vein, declaring it as his experience that he was happier for every additional guinea of income that he got. We may misuse wealth, but deliverance from anxiety is felt, when it comes, to be a blessing which cannot be gainsaid.

There is one consideration, however, for restless imaginations, busy in amending the arrangements of Providence. No one living has a right to believe himself or those about him independent of circumstances. Men's wants and deficiencies have a large part in the formation of the purest and most disinterested friendships, and even in maintaining them. If our friends' worldly condition were materially improved, we cannot be at all sure that they would be the same to us. It is highly improbable that they would. We fit one another as we are. Very likely some element of unfitness would spring up if our relative positions were altered. Our society may now be invested with some subtle charm of sympathy for which then there would be no play. Or our friend would have other claims more importunate than ours, in which we must acquiesce if we are wise, but which would not the less make a change where change is not welcome. Perhaps the charm and sentiment of our lives — what is, after all, better to us, and more indispensable than material wealth — hangs on our being no richer, no more prosperous, no more independent than we are. If, then, there is anything in our relations with others that we cling to, and could not bear to see altered, we had best, even in this matter of wanting money, cheerfully reconcile ourselves to the universal need, and, because there is something we care for more, make ourselves content and satisfied with things as they are.